ACTUALITY
infinity at play

Amaya Gayle

Other books by Amaya Gayle:

The Grand Experiment: An Expedition of Self-Discovery

Workplace Evolution: Common Sense for Uncommon Times

Silent Presence: Grief's Unfolding Promise

Riding the Tornado's Tail: 20 Stories from Caregivers Who Have Been There

The Wild Child, a pocketbook and companion oracle deck

Publisher's Note

This publication is designed to provide accurate and authoritative information in regard to the subject matter covered. It is sold with the understanding that the publisher is not engaged in rendering psychological, financial, legal, or other professional services. If expert assistance or counseling is needed, the services of a competent professional should be sought.

Copyright © 2024, 2026 Amaya Gayle

First published by New Sarum Press, April 2024

ISBN 979-8-90271-180-3

All Rights Reserved

Table of Contents

Terms used in this book xi
Chapter 1 • Vanished … adrift in the search 1
    You can't unring that bell 2
    Leaving everything behind 2
    Mind couldn't understand 3
    Trapped 4
    So what was real for me? 4
    Torn between sane and crazy, but which is which? 5
    If only it was simple … but maybe it is 6
    Not-twoness, nothing, non-separation 6
    The body and the felt sense 7
    A guide? 7
    The word is not the thing 8

Chapter 2 • Inconceivable 9
    Is truth knowable? 9
    Conscious or not, you are tired of pretending 10
    Can *you* hear it? That sound is you cracking open 11
    No need to look for the path 12
    Life isn't what you think it is 12
    You know you want to find out 13
    Outside the zone of conformity 13
    Don't just believe me 14
    The status quo—is it as safe as it feels? 14
    You choose … or so it seems 15
    Life is the big reveal 15
    Drink the living water 16
    Beliefs are self-replenishing 16
    There is no end to discovery 17

Chapter 3 • One Tiny Problem 18
- I wanted what they had … 18
- … it's a trap 19
- One tiny problem … 19
- No enemies 'out there' 20
- The many-headed myth that is … 20
- … the separate self 21
- Meantime … don't put me down 21
- Seeing past the myth, seeing through the dream and… 22
- … Seeing it as it is 23

Chapter 4 • Blueprint 24
- Is the world personal? 24
- The personal—an inner blueprint 24
- Do you want to know why the world is as it is? 25
- Fabrications of a fabricated mind 25
- Are you ready to see what life really is? 26
- The separate self will lead you 26
- What you hold onto defines reality for you 27
- Merciful life … 27
- My way isn't everyone's highway 29
- There may be no success like failure 29
- Experience just as it is, is the teacher 30

Chapter 5 • Why bother? 31
- So what if the world is not what it seems—is it a big deal? .. 31
- Can you choose this? 32
- 'Progress' 32
- Feeling the pull … 33
- … and you know there's no stopping it 33
- Bliss: often a requirement but never a destination 34

The truth or the trappings—which do you want?................35
Predestination ... who wants to know? 35
In a world of infinite possibilities..............................36
Could anything be different from what it is? 36
Are you ready to see?..37
A collision course with delusion..................................38
A time of quickening..39
Incarnation—why bother?..41

Chapter 6 • Experiencing..43
What is experience? 43
Can you see the inherent freedom? 44
Snips and snails and puppy dog tails 44
Where do *you* stop and *I* begin? 45
If there isn't a storyline are *you* still present? 45
What is that *I*, the one who experiences life?.............. 46
Experiencing—get out of your head and into your life.........47
It is not nothing—it's infinity at play 48
Fallacies abounding 48
You have never needed to be saved 49

Chapter 7 • Thoughts Do Not Think................................ 51
One thought at a time? Not so!..................................52
Don't let double vision fool you 52
Eventually the dam must break 53
Don't believe a word I write ... find out for yourself..............54
Empty space isn't empty 55
Simply notice...56
You are not doing the thinking; aliveness is thinking *you*....57

Chapter 8 • Cause and Effect 58
- Finding the 'true cause' is the ultimate game 59
- Yikes! Can I have a different answer? 59
- Blaming—it's primal! 60
- Avoidance tactics—have they ever changed *What Is*? 61
- 'No cause'—a scary idea? 62
- What if you are staging your own reality show? 62
- Who is to blame for all this? No one! 63

Chapter 9 • Not Knowing 64
- Do you think knowing will save you? 64
- What makes you think you need to be saved? 65
- As soon as you know anything … 66
- Certainty is not the antidote … it's the toxin itself............. 66
- Life itself is your mirror 67
- You are the resurrection 68

Chapter 10 • Patience … Wait for It 70
- Surrender isn't a bargain to get a better life.........................70
- Needing to know is an attempt to manipulate the flow 71
- Can you find a time when you chose your thoughts? 71
- Dance, baby, dance! 72
- It's always been in your blood 75
- A kindergarten simulation...76

Chapter 11 • Time and Space—There Goes the World......77
- Progress: a concept?..78
- Life: a speculation? 78
- Time: a mental construct?...79
- Do you want to be thrilled? Then stay tuned!...................... 80
- The spacetime cookie crumbles 81

Chapter 12 • The Wow of Now 83
Now: not a snippet of time 83
How could you not be present? 84
The prison door swung wide 85
Finding your way out of the optical illusion 85
The killer question 86
How old are you when you don't look in the mirror? 86

Chapter 13 • Silence and Stillness 88
What exactly is mind? 89
Who does the thinking? 89
Are your thoughts entertaining, disconcerting—or both? .. 90
Pitfalls on the path 91
If it is possible to control thought, why can't you? 92
Experiencing: the direct route 92
Silence vs quiet 93
Your experience is dynamite! 94
You are the switch that flips 94

Chapter 14 • Feeling 96
Where do you stash your monsters? 97
Does separation blunt the pain? (The answer is *No*!) 97
Fear not! Breathe life in and *feel*! 98
Are you ready to see your fear? 101
Whatever arises ... meet that 101
What's real? 103
Feeling the darkness reveals what the darkness is 103

Chapter 15 • The Persistent Myth of Choice 105
Not choosing—still a choice 105
Life is *doing life* 107

Why? Why? Why? 107
The infinitely evolving blueprint chooses..........................108
Would you really choose the bad stuff? Honestly?.............108
Is anyone really in charge?..109

Chapter 16 • Incarnation—Reincarnation 111
Life after death, or life after life? 112
Splintered truths: life and death.. 113
Beware of pre-packaged truth... 114
If there is no time, what does that mean for immortality?.. 114

Chapter 17 • Futility 116
Are you there yet? Have you reached the
point of futility? 117
If you do still have hope—don't despair! 118
Do you really know what you're going to do next? 118
Tough times are pregnant with possibility........................... 119
Dreams always point..120
If it's grabbing your attention, then pay attention 121
You can still live a brilliant life.. 122

Chapter 18 • Preferences, Do They Matter?.................... 123
Embrace those teaching moments in your life....................124
Do you listen to your body? 125
Avoidance doesn't work for long.. 125
Noticing is magic in motion 127

Chapter 19 • A Bad Rap 128
You are so much more than you think 129
Are you looking for an escape ramp?.................................130

Chapter 20 • Default Patterns..132
- How do you make yourself small?..133
- Have you noticed your default yet?......................................133
- Breaking open—like life—is often hard.............................134
- There's no one to blame..135
- How could energy ever be separated?.................................136
- Olly olly oxen free!..137

Chapter 21 • Dance of Polarities..138
- Wouldn't it be nice if life behaved the way you want..........139
- There's no expansion without contraction..........................140
- Searching for truth or hunting for gold...............................141
- Yes is the only word you need..141

Chapter 22 • Dream a Little Dream..................................144
- So it's a dream—is that all bad?..145
- What a fabulous bargain of a lifetime!.................................146
- In what ways are you hanging on?.......................................146

Chapter 23 • The End of the Endgame............................148
- Is there such a thing as truth?...149
- Letting go of the dream … from within the dream............150
- Do you question the givens in your life?.............................151
- What if comfort is over-rated?...152
- If the world were really a dream—would it be so bad?......153
- Just because it's a dream doesn't make life less appealing...153

Chapter 24 • The Hope of Awakening..............................155
- Judgment: a good indicator that you are still on the wheel..156
- Would you really want that ultimate escape?.....................157
- Phew! Dodged that bullet!..158

You are filled with relief, but what has changed?.................158
Everything is; nothing is not 159
You are so much more than whatever you believe 160

Chapter 25 • Does Love Always Win? 162
What is your sense of this? Does love always win? 162
What do you mean by love? 163
When life seems unfathomable 164
Your brokenness wants to be seen 165
If you recognized *what you are*..166

Chapter 26 • Resisting Resistance 168
… and we've circled back around to experiencing 169
An intellectual, mind-only understanding 170
Are you genuinely willing to explore your beliefs 171
It won't feel safe. Safety is an idea composed of threaded thoughts.. 172

Chapter 27 • Death Throes 174
There's a dragonfly in my cosmic soup 175
Death opens a door you can walk right through 175
Death is a pointer, not a dead end......................................176

Chapter 28 • Perception of Light 178
Clear away ideas and beliefs so that you can see 179
It's tricky...180
Skip the show and go straight to experiencing 181
Even though it's not real in the way you think 182
You are magnificence itself … 182

About Amaya Gayle.. 185

Terms used in this book

The following words are not intended to add more certainty or beliefs to your stockpile. Seeing that possibility, I hesitated to compile this list, but acknowledged that working definitions might be of benefit to those not familiar with the words or how I use them. Each term on the list points to *Infinite Aliveness*, not to something you can stick a pin through and put in your pocket. Others may use these words differently. This list is simply how I used them for the purpose of this book.

Actuality
The dance of *Infinite Aliveness*: the felt-sense of separation simultaneously appearing out of that which could never be separate. Actuality is *What Is* regardless of recognition, denial or ignorance.

Appearance
A term pointing to the possibility that life isn't actually solid and material, limited and definable. Even though the appearance is wholly convincing, life may simply appear to be composed of individuated people and things, discrete objects in a seemingly discrete world.

Awakened
Clearly, irreversibly realizing what life is; also called enlightened or realized.

Awareness/
Consciousness
Everything is energy, the movement of aliveness taking form and releasing it, including your body and its wounds, its openness, and all apparent points in between. It is called many names: energy—consciousness—awareness—isness, all words for simple, basic experiencing, experiencing that is unconditional, that does not preclude any experience. Nothing could be excluded in the one that is not-two.

Experiencing
There is only one experience—fundamental experiencing—all-inclusive, the one without another. Experiencing is overlooked, underestimated, and ignored. We ignore what we don't understand, what we don't value. Giving experiencing its due, recognizing its omnipotence, is markedly more precise than battling beliefs.

Infinite Aliveness
What is here right now—Life—is *Infinite Aliveness*, *Awareness* masquerading as loss and ache, imprisonment and grief, as every storyline of humanity's chains and joys.

Non-duality—Actuality
A simple, yet easily misunderstood and misused term, that points to *Actuality*, to what life actually is. It is also a philosophy based on the non-existence of separation.

Not-two
Life is often described as oneness, but the idea of one cannot help but allow for the fallacious assumption of two, three, or

more. Not-two means *Actuality: This That Is* before and beyond ideas of divisible and indivisible while including the appearance of them.

Presence
The divine paradox is never absent. It is always present, for it is *Presence* itself. It is the nature of experience, the surprisingly ordinary holy fractal graphic display, the view of separation as the *Actuality* of not-two.

Separation/Duality
The common, mostly unquestioned belief in materialism that confirms life is made of finite, separate objects—you, me, the world—things that are born and will die.

This
All that seemingly Is and is not, the mystery and the apparently knowable, the invisible and the visible.

CHAPTER 1

Vanished ... adrift in the search

One day I found myself on a path I didn't intend to walk. There was no surprise, no fanfare—it just happened. I couldn't even figure out, at least without a fair bit of contemplation, which fork in the road I had taken to get me there, but I had a sense that I'd been stumbling around on it for a while. Amidst a broad sweep of success and failure, happiness and joy, life still hurt. My wounds were festering rather than healing, so I began walking down roads looking for answers that I wouldn't have considered before.

I vividly remember the day I noticed that the down-to-earth woman I'd been had vanished without a trace into the spiritual search. It wasn't something I consciously chose. It seemed to have chosen me, but I didn't understand that at the time. I just knew that things that had been important, that were fundamental to most humans, weren't important anymore. I had stepped into a maze and no longer cared whether or not I could find my way out. I may have assumed I could retrace my steps, and slowly carefully quietly back out, but I didn't try. That would have been worse than being stuck in the maze forever.

You can't unring that bell

I couldn't unsee what I had seen. I'd had a few glimpses of something beyond the beliefs I'd inherited. The rigidity those beliefs imposed on me itched to burst open. I didn't even know which of the quick looks had taken hold, threatening to uproot generations of rules and values, twisting the outer and inner paths into something foreign, unrecognizable. I still don't know. Maybe it was simply a cumulative effect and I'd reached my own hundredth monkey. Whatever it was, I'd seen enough that it was no longer possible for me to believe what I'd once taken to be true.

I suspected the price would be steep, stripping away everything I held dear. No one would consciously choose that, at least not anyone in their right mind. But that's the deal. Somewhere on the path the 'right mind' is lost, seen to be a composite of all the little checkboxes that came before. I knew the way I lived wasn't *it*, but I didn't know what *it* was. I couldn't go back, but I didn't know where to step next.

Leaving everything behind

I couldn't even explain why. It was just an inner knowing. I left behind people I loved, friends and family that couldn't go—wouldn't go—where I was going. They were on their own path and their path was not mine. It would have been nice to know that all paths eventually converge. At the time, it felt like one impossibly brutal loss after another, and in many ways it was—with the exception of the most important one.

Walking along, not knowing where to go, I encountered detours and dead-ends and picked up the idea that separation was the villain in the piece. It was the one common thread so

I deduced that all those talking it up, and down, had to be right ... or so I thought. I began trying to get around separation, but everywhere I looked, there it was. I knew I was missing something, but I couldn't figure out what it was.

Mind couldn't understand

It certainly appeared that I lived in a physical world made of matter. It was filled with billions of things and distinct physical beings who have a beginning and end. There was a definite sense of being a separate self. It seemed that the belief in *more than one* was valid. It didn't appear to be an ideation composed of programmed mental certainty coupled with the felt sense of *thingness*, of being a body. Ideation? No, it was real ... it had to be. But separation was the boogey man in spirituality, that which must be overcome. It wasn't an assumption based on theory, unprovable at that, or was it?

I listened to spiritual talks, and if you have too, you've likely heard the word *separation* as well. It's right up there with *ego:* that which shall not be allowed to survive. Teachers and gurus, students and followers, beginners and those who've been around the circuit awhile, not to mention some who don't identify as spiritual at all, use both terms frequently, and very often quite differently.

With all the different versions it's hard to definitively pin the villain down or maybe I was just too caught in my beliefs to listen deeply enough. What I came to realize though, was that each definition was built around the degree of separation experienced by the speaker, the particular brand of power animating their ego, which only managed to add contradiction rather than clarification.

Trapped

The spiritual quest attracts a mishmash of information, like one of those signposts with arrows pointing in twenty different directions. The mixed messages are pretty hard to miss if you are paying attention. The definitions seemed to attempt to convert shiny new beliefs into solid reality, an appearance of truth into an absolute, and for me at least, they added to the confusion rather than illuminating the dysfunction I was trying to escape. How could I get out of the trap I was in if I didn't know what tripped it in the first place? People who proclaimed that they *knew the truth* seemed more like they were putting a wide net over smoke and mirrors, expecting me to find their prescribed reflection caught in the mesh.

The only thing I could come up with was that as long as I was here, separation would be too, so it must be me that was the problem. That led me round another bend in the maze, a new escape route out of the problem: the ego must go. If only I'd understood what I do now. I could have saved myself a lot of time and heartache ... but I didn't.

So what was real for me?

At its most elemental level, I experienced the sense of separation as a simple boundary between me and life. I used to think that boundary was my skin. Inside the skin was *me*. Outside was *you* and the rest of the world. I didn't consider whether mind and soul were included or separate too. I hadn't gotten that far yet. Is the body, mind, and soul whole, non-separated, or not? I didn't know. I didn't even think it was important. This thing, the *me* thing, whether that meant the triune me or not, looked and felt like it was separate from all other things.

All of it existed in a finite world of matter. Each thing was discrete, independent, distinct, with a limited shelf life. Separation, in that sense, was another name for limitation, for death.

That wouldn't have been a problem for me, the seeker I was, if it hadn't been so obviously accurate. It was tricky to discern any other viewpoint, to see what's really here, because I still believed what I'd been taught. I believed in separation. I didn't see what I see now. I didn't consider the space between things as part of the whole—now I would ask where would life be without that space? I didn't understand awareness, nowness, hereness were all the same thing and that they weren't really a thing … or a place … or some esoteric concept. I thought I had at least a modicum of control even though I was pretty ineffective at wielding it with any consistency. I thought so many things and I didn't truly know anything.

Torn between sane and crazy, but which is which?

Dangling from the web of separation, I experienced a life of duality: of black and white, me and you, us and them, heaven and earth, material and ethereal, and therein found sustaining proof of my basic assumption. I wasn't at fault. There was no one to blame. Most people, except the wildly crazy ones, believe separation is reality, that we are individualized physical beings living in a material world, so it wasn't something I missed, that I should have seen.

I didn't know that crazy was what I sought. It was also what I desperately tried to avoid. At times the dissonance felt like it was tearing me apart.

Perhaps my story sounds familiar.

No matter how long you seek, or how hard you try, hanging onto separation, consciously or not, cannot but create the experience of isolation, alienation, and aloneness, for that is its very essence. The pain that naturally arises in separation's wake is foundational to the quest. The fallacious self, the self who is made entirely of ideas and beliefs, is the same one who seeks the separate self's demise.

It's quite the enigma.
Nothing is as it seems.

If only it was simple ... but maybe it is

Non-separation, not-twoness, is not what I thought either. It is not the opposite of separation, nor is it separation pieced together, the sum of the parts. It's so much more than simple interconnectedness. Oh, if only it were that easy! It is easy, but not in the way you think while spinning around in separation.

I'll cut to the end of the story, although it will be nothing more than ideas until your life exposes itself for what *This* actually is. Not-twoness includes everything, and everything means everything, and that includes nothing. Exclusion happens. It's part of the story. It gets to be included too. Non-separation is inclusive of all things, including the appearances that you would like to banish to the hottest regions of hell. It's not as straightforward as the split mind would like, but it certainly isn't complicated. Cut anything out of non-separation, snip off even the smallest piece and you experience separation.

Not-twoness, nothing, non-separation

Non-separation is the foundation of our being. It is the undivided natural state, if it could be called a *state*. It isn't a state

—but that's a story for later. Separation is division, splitting apart, comparing and contrasting. It's an unnatural way for us to live. It's also what causes you to ache with desire for something else.

All that is known, and can be known, is included.

Not-twoness is not a high-minded ideal. It is not an ideal a mind can understand. Rather, it is a felt sense, or at least what we humans experience as a result of having a body. In the material world you don't simply see and feel, you are sensing and perceiving no matter whether you are residing in separation, or are in on the cosmic joke.

The body and the felt sense

When you experience the world through a body there is a felt sense. When you die, all bets are off, but you'll have to actually die to know for certain. When you see the world as separate, you feel separate with all the appended concerns, fears, and doubts. When that separation is seen through, when *Actuality* is clearly apparent, the felt sense shifts. Once that is the case, even when we use separation to navigate the seemingly material world, there is an effortlessness, with a shift back when the illusion is no longer useful.

A guide?

There are challenges in being a seeker for truth, especially when, like many seekers, you equate truth with escaping separation. How can you know if the guide you are trusting with your heart has actually seen through the fallacy of separation. What if you can't know?

Looking through the lens of separation, wouldn't you perceive everyone you meet as functioning from separation, whether they are or not? It won't be clear. You'll have doubts and questions. Looking outside for confirmation will not work.

It might seem to work for a little while, but it won't last. That little twist adds a level of exquisite complexity to the challenge, which will only enhance the inherent mystery as you are, or will be, discovering for yourself. It's a big part of the fun.

What would life be without its living obstacle course?

Nothing.

The word is not the thing (and the map is not the territory)

Reading the words won't guide you through the maze, not while you still feel separate, not while you believe what you see, and what you see is a world of separation. It's got you coming and going, but something within you is saying that life is not what it seems, so these words can act as a homing beacon or a flashing pointer. Whether it makes sense or not—and no, it doesn't make sense—nothing is going to stop you from moving further into the maze.

CHAPTER 2

Inconceivable

Disclaimer: No words are ultimately true. Words by their very nature are limited. They are finite expressions forged in the fires of duality. Attempts to put *Actuality* into words will fail, for reality is unimaginably inconceivable. Having seen the inherent comedy, the arrogance in thinking it is possible, I no longer try, but I do love to play, to point, to add to the conversation as honestly as I can. At best, words get you to the neighborhood; whether or not you recognize the address is not up to you, even though it definitely appears it should be. It is up to trillions of pinpoints of information coalescing as you and the world.

Is truth knowable?

With this baseline, how can you know the ultimate truth? Perhaps the idea of truth is overrated and overstated. Who looks for it anyway? Truth has no need to look for itself. If you drop the appearances of body and world, all that's here is expression, energetic inputs and outputs, reactive stimuli, perpetual motion, seemingly endeavoring to define itself, to make itself known, evoking thoughts, stirring emotions, coloring perceptions, teasing sensations, utilizing words—the activity of exquisitely fundamental experiencing.

The attempts and inevitable failures, the joy of unfettered experimentation, of seeing what touches us gently enough to coax open a heart and what fails to connect, is a grand feature of this simulation, a precious aspect of the dream, adding depth and richness, facilitating the search and begging discovery. Hiding in plain sight, while not really hiding at all, it is the nature of *This That Is* to be discovered, to shower us with its recognizable inconceivability.

Conscious or not, you are tired of pretending

Maybe that's the reason we want to be seen for who we really are, why we are so tired of pretending, of making believe we are something we are not, of aspiring to be other than what we are. We too, are the inconceivability begging discovery.

Finite beings aren't built to conceive infinite possibilities. The finite separate self is the antithesis of *Actuality*. Luckily, you aren't finite. Yes, life unquestionably appears to be limited materiality, but it is not finite in any way.

The world, and what you call life, is nothing but *Infinite Aliveness*. There is no separation at all, even when veiled by the distortion of belief. Believing something is so, even if it appears to be so, does not make it true.

Words hold the potential to be valuable pointers in a world certain of its agreed-upon reality: the dualistic view of subject and object, inherent separation and physically dependent consciousness. Whether words point to further distortion of the truth, or an expression nearer reality is experienceable, but that experience cannot be labeled and put in a book, no more than you can know the taste of an orange by looking at a picture. Truth is not simply beyond words, it is beyond thought, the springboard for all words, and the concept of truth is but another thought, another word. Truth is separation's concept.

Can *you* hear it? That sound is you cracking open

Even the most unclouded words can only point to a version, albeit a less separation-saturated version, of quintessential aliveness ... and still, they are wondrously capable of opening a crack in the armor and triggering direct experience. How amazing! In that sense, words are quite magical. When they take us into our exquisite experience, they implore us to look with wide open eyes and a welcoming heart.

Infinite Aliveness needs no truth, no definition, no words, and no one to believe in it. It doesn't require perfection, a stripping away of all belief, or an empty vessel to pour its richness into the world. It simply is, and quite surprisingly to many, it is the inconceivable mystery and the entirely conceivable material world, for they are not-two.

To glimpse life's marvelous eccentricity, to grok what you are and see past the ruse of separation, you cannot simply set down your beliefs and will yourself to quit defending them. You cannot unbelieve what you believe. You believe what you believe no matter how many affirmations you say, how many replacement words and phrases you use, and how many times you tell yourself you don't ... and that only speaks to conscious beliefs. Most beliefs are buried under layers of embedded assumption masquerading as established fact.

No need to look for the path—it's your perfectly ordinary life

Fortunately, the unraveling of belief isn't something the believer does. The doing (were you to call it that) requires the guidance and guise of your perfectly ordinary messy experience, life with all its ups and downs.

Life is the undoing.

You journey down a path made just for you and your inimitable odyssey, the path appearing as your remarkable life. Embodiment is the guise you wear, *you* the sparkling dynamic presence, *This That Is: Experiencing—Consciousness—Awareness—Isness—Actuality*. If you could squeeze those words together into one, one that is not five, one that holds not the merest smidgen of two-ness, it would be closer to the mark, for they are interchangeable with not a bit of difference between them. They all point to the one.

Life isn't what you think it is

Your experience of life often falls short of sparkling aliveness, not because it isn't infinitely vital, dynamically aware, but because you are conditioned to take the false as true and the true as false. You are unintentionally adept at the separation game, and that blinds you to what is right in front of your eyes, right here, right now playing out through the glimmer of perception and sensation, the shimmer of thought and emotion.

Every single thing you assume you know, that you take to be true, blocks the experience of reality as it actually is. You believe a lot of things, all of them verifiably relative, by nature limited, and lacking even a smidge of substance. So long as you are holding any belief you cannot notice what this is, what you are, and as a natural consequence, you experience reality as you think it is: a life of frustration, betrayal, and heartbreak, interspersed with fleeting moments of relief.

Many humans act primarily from unconsciousness. You are not alone, you are not the only one who has fallen for the subterfuge. It is the human condition and when we fall for it we call it *consensus reality*. Without questioning, you accept that the way you believe life to be is actually the way it is, and happily, you are profoundly mistaken.

You know you want to find out

It would be rather silly and quite impudent of me to tell you what to do, to give you a technique or practice—God forbid—to add another belief to your already overflowing load. Until those beliefs are shaken, broken open and laid out for clear viewing, they will continue to shape the narrative that underpins and colors your experience.

Life is the breaking open, the organic unraveling. It is quite natural, but you've been raised in a world that, with the exception of a few rare beings, fails to question the fallacious beliefs obscuring reality. The legacy of unquestioned lies makes the process of recognition damnably painful, when in fact the ongoing disclosure is supremely ordinary and purely inescapable. Disclosure is taking place—that's what life is—and because to question reality is frowned upon, it feels like being tumbled in a mile-high wave rather than the cleansing caress of a gentle rain.

Outside the zone of conformity

Questioning, feeling, and experiencing life, rips off the veil, the veil installed by a knowing world. The fathomless reality is now revealed: you are the elemental, immutable peace and happiness you seek. The misinformation that you, and all humans, have been indoctrinated with cloaks the indisputable realization that calls off the search and ends all questions as to your worth.

It is easy to see why a society that thrives on war and discontent would find no reason to embrace such ideas; it would call them insane and then subsidize the distortion.

Don't just believe me ...

Saying *you are already what you seek* doesn't have any substantive weight when that is not your reality. When life feels anything but peaceful and happy and the world is fixated on fixing you, such phrases don't have any purchase. Until the inseparable is experienced as a felt sense, a deep and undeniable recognition, the idea that you were never separate is relegated to the garbage heap, or closeted in the land of woo—the realm of fairytales.

It would be doing you no favors though, to point to your current operating system as real, to speak from it as if it were actual, to lend credence to the system of invalidation that makes you feel lacking and in need of being fixed. To say that is what you are, to go along with the charade, would be a tragedy, for it is the great lie.

The status quo—is it as safe as it feels?

If you thirst to recognize what you are, what this is, take heart. It need not take years, let alone lifetimes. Your life is already the unraveling realization. Feeling into what is demonstrable, the essence of experiencing, making direct contact with what is actually present, cannot help but reveal what you are, what this is, for it was never hidden.

Shifting focus from the contents of experience—the entire focus of materiality—to experiencing itself, is not in the status quo's playbook; it is based on the rules you currently follow. Intent on the contents, on what looks important, you skip past what experiencing really is. You go to the movie, and utterly dismiss the verifiable fact of the screen. It's not important, is it? Well, yes. It is.

You choose ... or so it seems

You either continue down the well-worn, unsatisfactory path that most humans tread, or you open yourself to new possibilities no matter how outside the norm they seem. Instead of assigning a reality to life's contents that in fact does not exist, you question reality itself and see what it shows you.

It is possible to let the misinformation that drives you just lie. You let it lie until it buries itself. Not an easy ask. Good thing you don't have to do it. You can't; your experience is doing it for you.

Life is the big reveal

What you are, what this is, cannot be disguised forever. Nothing remains as it is. Eventually, life shows you that what you think you know is not trustworthy, so celebrate the hard knocks that bring you to your knees. You never know which event will be the grace-filled prod that impregnates your experience with sacred suspicion. It seems to take a gentle push—or untold stronger ones—to trigger enough curiosity to pierce the chainmail of knowing.

What this actually is cannot be put into a tight box of

understanding. It cannot be taught linearly in a seminar, or be found in a how-to book. Knowing is part of the illness, not the remedy. The truth lives within you. Humans throughout the ages have strangled the inklings of aliveness that brought them relief, that resonated within their hearts, until the sparkling dynamic presence that sparked the recognition was demoted to dogma and set down in ink on paper.

Drink the living water

Words that direct you to something outside of your immediate experience are not genuine pointers, but misguided manipulation cloaked in loving guidance. Your experience, the actual context and content of now, your verifiably precious dreadful joyful hard life is the powerful force that cracks open eons of falsehoods. No one can give you this. No one can give you something you already have, that you already are.

Beliefs are self-replenishing

Belief systems have limitless layers of distortion. Rather than diminishing as each layer is seen, they automatically replenish themselves. Thus, wrestling with your beliefs, seeing through them in hopes of undoing them, will always be an ill-fated undertaking.

Providentially, there is only one experience—fundamental experiencing—all-inclusive, the one without another. Experiencing is generally brushed aside or dismissed outright. We tend to have little regard for what we don't understand, what we don't respect. Seeing experiencing for what it is, recognizing its brilliant pervasiveness, is markedly more effective than battling beliefs that automatically refresh.

There is no end to discovery

When you realize the true nature of experience it is not the end, it doesn't mean you're home free. It is more of a foundational shift, a shift from being lost in a fog of fallacy to walking towards the light of *Actuality*. There are many waystations upon life's byways, places you will still be tempted to set up shop. The known territory gives off a siren call, a call that imitates the temptations of the Christ. There is always further, another knot unraveling, something new to discover.

Every experience is an opportunity to taste unfiltered experiencing, to let a peach-colored rose entice your senses, to pluck a blade of grass and taste its greenness, to watch in awe as a fat robin flies overhead, for aliveness to permeate each aspect of your life.

Every single experience is life reaching out, tugging at your heart, doing what life does, reeling you in, calling you home, asking you to feel, to *see*.

When you are truly willing to let life be, to see it, to feel it as it is, rather than seeing and feeling your beliefs about it, when you are ready to experience what's here without reservations, to live as *Actuality*, you will see what you have missed.

CHAPTER 3

One Tiny Problem

I wanted what they had ...

Turn over any rock and you'll find someone who has found what you are looking for, who has what you want. At first glance they seem serene, at peace. Some even appear to be floating rather than walking through this pain-filled world.

Who wouldn't want that? Heaven knows I did, especially when the pain felt stuck and beyond repair.

As the fear ramps up and the world catches fire it seems everyone has something to sell, a technique to speed awakening, a sweet yet powerful breakthrough meditation, a new way to eat that will raise your resonance, one-on-one coaching to help you find yourself, group intensives to crack you open, people of a like mind to share the journey with and all-important pointers to people you should avoid.

Almost every technique being sold is a denial of your inherent beauty, a fix for your brokenness. It is self-flagellation, more of the same, only cleaned up, sanitized, fit for today's data-laden consumer. It is what you've been fed your entire life, what you say to yourself at 3 am on a sleepless night ... *something is wrong with me.*

... it's a trap

That one destructive idea is the be-all and end-all prerequisite for the get-out-of-pain self-improvement awakening story, and someone other than you must have the remedy, because God knows you don't.

Venture far enough into this trap and you figure out that you not only don't have the remedy, but you are the problem, your ego, your *I don't need, won't get anyone's help* stance, the *me-me-me* human. You tell yourself that the separate self—a useless, worthless impediment—must be overcome. Its desires, needs, beliefs—all those things that make you separate—annihilated. You must kill the Buddha and the Buddha is you.

So you meditate, find bliss and lose it, generally not long after the meditation, the group gathering or the retreat ends ... or sooner if someone happens to say something that rips off a scab covering one of your untended wounds. You eat less meat, no meat, nothing with a face. You chant and practice. Your friends drift away, or you simply quit attending to them. Eventually, your spiritual-enough bullshit meter is so fine-tuned that nothing and no one can pass through.

You find yourself alone, doing the work. Of course you are alone. That's necessary, isn't it?

And the pain is still present, if anything, more present, and you scream at the heavens: *Just kill me already! Annihilate me! I do not care if I die; God, I am so tired of being separate and alone.*

One tiny problem ...

All desires to annihilate the separate self are the stuff of fantasy, a flying pig. In truth, the pig has a better chance of taking wing than the seeker does of escaping the separate self. The separate self is the seeking, the resistance to life, the need for annihilation. It is also a necessary and useful appearance on the board game of life.

How much easier it would be if there actually was an enemy to defeat, something to overcome, and perhaps most importantly, someone to do it!

Give you a war and you know what to do, even if it is just a child's sandbox war. You have been trained for that from the beginning.

The messed up overwrought crumbling planet you currently live on is a projection of that same desire for annihilation, as is the messed up over-medicated warring world and its lost and lonely inhabitants.

No enemies 'out there'

If you only knew the truth of this place and yourself everything would flip on its back for a little belly rub.

There isn't an enemy out there—that's the bad news. The far worse news is there isn't an enemy within.

There is no one to fight. There is no separate self, no egoic self, no separate other, no separate world at all. There is nothing wrong and no one to fix it if there were.

All your struggles are fights against the ghosts of imagination, paper tigers in the concrete jungle, and the more you struggle, the more razor-sharp teeth you encounter.

The many-headed myth that is …

The separate self is the mythical hydra. Cut one head off and two more appear, only this hydra does not have the power of regeneration. That power lies in your incredible imagination.

Experiencing your improvisational stories makes them feel real because experiencing lends them the sniff of truth: sensation, perception, thought, and emotion. It gives them the buzz and tingle of reality. There is but the appearance, the seen and felt sense of separation, which I admit is more than enough to instill the desire to war, to win, to escape, but the separate self, the villain in the piece, is nothing you can overcome, transcend, or annihilate. It is a Gordian knot, an intractable problem—the problem which does not exist. This non-existent reality is the knot at the center of the tight wound, the heart ache that is the separate self.

… the separate self

The separate self is an imaginary character in an equally imaginary world. The world is nothing if not its imaginary characters. What is required, what is sought, is not raising the victor's banner, a conquering hero of mythic proportion, but the recognition of what is truly going on, and that is not something you, the imaginary character, can do. You, the separate self, are imaginary after all—a very real illusion, a true and convincing mirage.

Meantime… don't put me down

Even though you are imaginary that does not mean life is a fraud, that our human appearance is somehow unimportant, or (heaven forbid!) something to quickly detour around or bypass. Quite the contrary. Your life, the real mirage, the sensual, sensory illusion, is the miracle of miracles, the vehicle for discovering, for experiencing what this actually is.

Until the moment of insight appears, heralding the willingness to see what this is, you will continue to find enemies and wars to fight at home, across the world, and within yourself. You will burn the world down in search of the cause of your pain, hoping for a salve for your gaping wounds, and none of the effigies you hang from the noose of your misguided imagination will bring you one step closer to what you seek. Until you recognize what life actually is, what you are, you are destined to fail.

Fortunately, that is not a bad thing, even though it may feel like hell.

Seeing past the myth, seeing through the dream and...

The common belief that this is a material reality, that you are a physical body inhabiting a physical world, living on a small blue ball spinning in one of countless galaxies, is at the heart of the dilemma. It is the *prima facie* stance springing from the fallacy of separation. That misconception is a result of your quite natural, outward-focused separation mentality.

A separate self cannot conceive of a world that is not comprised of separate things. In its ignorance, it makes of this phantasmagorical display a cheap copy, a graveyard of buried beauty.

This is not a material world. It is a world made from the stuff of experiencing; the same stuff dreams are made of. To the dreamed character there is no difference. The dream looks solid. It tastes and sounds solid. It even feels solid, but it is not, and when you wake up and lift your sleepy head off your pillow you remember that your dreamworld, while palpably real, while intricately detailed, was as unsubstantial as a mirage.

The waking world—the world you believe to be material—is no different. It is another dream, perhaps a slightly more convincing dream, although to be quite honest, nighttime dreams are pretty darn compelling.

Have you ever been startled awake from a dream unable to remember where you are? Did your heart pound so fast you thought it would explode before you remembered that the nightmare was not real? Afterwards, it takes hours to let it go, for it to dissolve into the truth of its ephemeral fragility.

... Seeing it as it is

Perhaps it was real, but real in a different way than you think. Maybe it is a real dream, an experienced illusion, just not materially founded.

What if that is life?
How do you know it isn't?
Wouldn't you like to know ... for sure?
You can prove it ...
You can prove it beyond even the illusory shadow of doubt.
Prove it and the search ends ...
... and the real fun begins.

CHAPTER 4

Blueprint

Is the world personal?

The world arises in and as *Infinite Aliveness*, not yours or mine as the scientific community would have you believe, but aliveness that is not broken in two, aliveness that is not personal, but infinite eternal experiencing: the appearance of the collectively personal and the personally collective, the inseparable expression of life.

The personal—an inner blueprint

You experience a personal world, the world created by a unique informational field, what I for lack of a better word call the *inner blueprint*. It's as good a phrase as any since words that point to the manifestation—and all words do—are supremely suspect and yet potentially helpful pointers, not to mention a source of wide-ranging entertainment.

Is it actually so, or even close? I'd counter that with *it's impossible to know*, but it is a great little concept that I find particularly useful. Everything known can trace its origins to what came before. No words are ever true or truly new, so the idea of blueprints, data fields, of you and the world for that matter, can never be more than a working model, a container of pointers spotlighting the sparkling gem you are.

In addition to the conceptual inner blueprint, your experience is informed by the precisely tuned blueprint of the shared world. Actually, they are not-two. Interestingly, the specifications, the blueprint that informs all models and beliefs—yours and the world's—are perpetually refreshed by those very same, yet ever-changing, models and beliefs. Life is not stagnant in any way, even though it may appear to be. It is a moving target impossible to pin down, to figure out. Grab ahold and like any good mirage, you find nothing there.

Do you want to know why the world is as it is?

The dynamic blueprint displays as the vital, ever-changing manifestation. If you want to know why the world is as it is, look within—not just within yourself but within the heart and mind, body and soul of all beings. The personal-collective field, the *Infinite Aliveness*, cannot but appear as you and the entirety.

What is fun and a little bent—okay, a lot—is the same aliveness, the only aliveness, that which isn't multiples, experiences life through the sensations, perceptions, thoughts, and emotions—the basic experiencing—of each apparently separate being.

Fabrications of a fabricated mind

You are both infinite and finite at the same time—well it would be the same time if time truly ticked. Time tick-tocks along one second at a time in the finite you and me world. It is a necessary construct, an assumed property of finitude—the world of duality, of separation—just like space. Neither is as we assume them to be. Both are fabrications of fabricated mind, requisite props for the experience of a lifetime. (More on time and space later).

Can you imagine any experience without space, a place for characters to walk and play, without that receptacle for worlds and universes, or without the continuity of time linking separate appearances together, without the myriad little things that combine and presume evidence of life? Nope, neither can I. Does that mean it is so? Not on your life.

Are you ready to see what life really is?

The view from separation is deceiving. The truth could be far beyond what any dreamed character is capable of understanding. The mystery is, after all, the mystery.

Once you are willing to consider that you might not know what's going on here, all that's left is to dive in heart-first and see what this actually *is*.

This need to see, this curiosity comes at a price—everything appears as a trade-off in the finite world.

Your usual way of seeing things withers away—its credibility is gone. The beliefs you put your faith and trust in, the identity you constructed for yourself—find themselves outside the door, no longer welcome guests This is done by life. It is not a doing, not something you can do. It is quite like packing up the toys of childhood as age redirects your interests.

The separate self will lead you

Everything is the movement, the activity of *Infinite Aliveness*. Your first steps down the lane of liberation are taken with the separate self's baggage in hand, seemingly spurred on by its fictitious needs and desires.

The desire for truth, for peace and happiness, appears as the desire of the separate self, although it, like all life, is the action of *Actuality*.

Those first steps arise in sync with mythical mind's yearning for an end to the pain and suffering, but it is life that scoots you forward, giving you experiences that open you further, that expand the horizon beyond what you can see. You either refuse the gift, wanting something different, or accept it and watch as your heavy anchors begin to unmoor. If you are sufficiently readied there is acceptance. If not, you will turn away until you are.

What you hold onto defines reality for you

Life isn't easy. You already know that. Anyone who says otherwise is far from reliable. The opening process is life, so it's not easy either, but when approached with curious willingness it becomes accessible. Once you trust what needs to happen, once you have seen that *knowing* stands in the way of *seeing*, it is less impossible to stand by as your pile of knowledge is shredded and you are emptied out. An organic letting-go is induced with the understanding that anything held onto is the filter that defines reality and defined reality obscures the view.

Merciful life …

When you look through eyes fitted with the lens of belief, you cannot see past what you think you know, what you believe, what feels important to hold onto. Mercifully, life has infinite ways to empty out the unmet experiences, the wounds and heartbreak you were incapable of feeling in the moment that catalyzed the beliefs. When you could not feel them directly, the flow was crystallized, imprisoning the hurts, the wounds, the sore and achy spots, inside you. Had you been able to meet them, to let them be without adding layers of story, they would have passed on by, leaving barely a trace, for they are simply data points swimming in the infinite field of life.

You can't though.

Life is growth and expansion: change, and that includes all expressions, those you meet with ease and those that cause you to shudder in resistance. Paradoxically, it's the ones that close us down tighter than a steel drum that offer the biggest openings.

The untended wounds, the unconsciously interrupted flow of life, leave you with a sense of being split, fractured, imperfect. That sense maintains your misplaced trust in lack and loss, in inadequacy, in separation.

Life is not capable of letting your assumed status quo be static, not even temporarily. Change is its nature. The ways it pries you open are as numerous as stars in the sky, for the pry bar is life itself. The experiences yet to come will redirect you, heal the brokenness, and end the war inside.

The processes and movements inside, seemingly waging an offensive to hold the line of that separate self, cannot but be undone. The inner discomfort you feel as this struggle takes place is an effective, yet painful, force of redirection. Life tends to direct you to whatever mode or method, book or practice, to whatever is right for you.

My way isn't everyone's highway

For me, redirection first took the form of meditation. It helped to loosen the cable anchoring me to what I deemed possible and true. I seemed to need meditation more than most, or maybe it just appeared that way to me. I did not trust life.

It took years of practice to make the tiniest dent in the shielding my custom-built armor provided. *Trust my experience? Are you kidding? Surrender to this? Hell, no!*

Meditation alone was not enough to stop me, to open my eyes so I could see what is here. It did its job, making it possible to stand in the middle of my experience without needing to run every time, but it took life's losses ... losing so many beloveds and coming face to face with my own death ... to prise my eyes wide open. I was a hard case. That doesn't mean you are too, or that your experience will be similar to mine.

There may be no success like failure

If the hope of a comfortable life, the gentle normalcy of friends and family, living to a ripe old age surrounded by loved ones—a householder's life—is the point of incarnation I would be considered a failure. Some of those I love might say I failed miserably. Perhaps I did, but it does not feel that way. Indeed, I have at times looked longingly at the world and wished for a bit of normal, right before I remember that normal is so far off my radar that I do not know what it is. If I could choose, I would still choose the life I have lived, that I am living, the traumas and losses for which I have grieved, the fear that has been met and seen through, the wounds that have festered and continue to heal.

Does that sound crazy? To me, the material world is crazy. In my storyline, consensus reality is insane. Sanity is understanding that this world is not what it seems, that this is not a material world but something else entirely.

Experience just as it is, is the teacher

To be consciously alive, to be aware that you are aliveness itself is invaluable, the Arkenstone of life. From where I stand, this bold and unique experiential tone is the vehicle of awakening, the one and only precious guru. There is no despair too deep, no shadow too dark, no heartbreak beyond limits, no price too steep to pay, for even the tiniest sliver of aliveness.

Recognizing what I now see, what would I tell my younger self to do, if even for just one glimpse?

> *Gladly ...*
> *unconditionally ...*
> *without a second thought ...*
> *risk it all!*

CHAPTER 5

Why bother?

What do you find in my words—futility or hope? If you could, it would be useful to choose futility. Hope holds out a carrot for something better and assumes a future that will never appear. I'm a big fan of futility. More on that later, too.

So what if the world is not what it seems—is it a big deal?

You are not what you seem. The world is not what it seems, and there is no way to win ... but that might not be so bad, so does it suck or not?

Why do the hard work if there's no way to slay the dragon? Why bother looking within if it doesn't change what's without? Why would anyone consciously dive deep into the shadow of self ... and is it absolutely necessary?

Those are all good questions, because doing the hard work isn't a lot of fun. Once started (it's always been in motion), it does not end until every single belief, every held trauma, every wisp of shrouded resistance to life as it is falls away. Falling is not quite accurate, at least for me it felt more like nails scraping a chalkboard sounds, but that was because I held on so tight. Maybe you won't be so pigheaded. Even if you're that lucky, it still won't be fun. Fun is not the word I would use. Anyone who tells you it is, who suggests blindly diving in, clearly does not know how deep the ocean trenches go, nor do they understand the reality of choice.

Can you choose this?

The good news and the bad news: it is not a choice. We are all doing the hard work, even when it doesn't seem like it. That is what life is—the hard work, unconscious for most, conscious for a few. Doing the work while unaware that you are *Infinite Aliveness* is life experienced as pain and suffering, frustration, doubt and anxiety with smatterings of hope and faith—the generally agreed-upon ragbag of reality.

When you feel that the work has become conscious you're on your way to base camp. Noticing it feels great. You put one boot in front of the other and say: *Woo hoo, I made it!* But you haven't realized that the trek up the summitless mountain still looms ahead.

'Progress'

Spiritual seekers tend to think in terms of progress and overstate their idea of headway. Every opening brings such relief that it's hard not to believe you've arrived. In comparison to the life that came before, it feels like you have. You're still in the dream, only the dream has changed from the revolving door of separation to what looks to be the path of ultimate escape. There's light at the end of the tunnel and it feels wonderful … until the next round begins.

Each opening comes with concomitant challenges, and each opening is different from the last. The harder you hold on the more painful it is. One day it would feel like having my balled-up fists ripped open, the next it felt like I was being consumed by deeply intense, concentrated energy that I couldn't identify. The more I resisted the worse it felt. See a theme? Each time, when I finally let go, when I could hold on no longer, when experience finally revealed what needed to be seen, something popped. I felt freer, expanded, open in ways I had not yet experienced.

Feeling the pull ...

That is the carrot and an enticing one it is. The sense of expansion is more addicting than sugar. It feels incredible. In comparison to what you called life before, this feels alive, like stepping onto a Technicolor set from a black and white waiting room.

I doubt you would keep going after the first time or two, even with the expansion bonus, if you had a choice. Heaven knows I wouldn't have. It feels dangerous, and to everything you've known it is. You would end the experiment and move on to something more fun, more fitting to your ideas of success.

In your search for peace and happiness, the true spiritual path—the dissection of all misdirection and patent lies—would have a little checkbox by it: Tried it. Didn't much like it. Next.

... and you know there's no stopping it

But you don't put a stop to it; you can't. Even though it seems like you choose, you are hooked after several fist-opening experiences and then you can't go back. Yeah, it's hard. It is painful. It cracks you open, spills your tears, but man oh man, the feeling afterwards: pure ambrosia.

The design, if you could call it that, is brilliant.

On the road into hell, if it is in your cards to go all the way in this go-around, you first become a seeker of bliss. Bliss is intoxicating. It draws you in and locks the exit. If you happen to find a teacher who showers love and light, that is their perfect part of this life gig—placing love's needle in your vein, feeding the addiction so that you are nicely hooked and cannot look away.

Many remain there, devoted to the high, without need to move on or reason why. Upgrading their beliefs, one set bartered for another, fear is exchanged for the love that heals. It's not a bad swap.

Bliss: often a requirement but never a destination

The bliss phase is a requirement for all but the rare soul. People have been known to awaken to *Actuality* after a night of drugs and alcohol, unaware that love and light even existed—a bit of a shocker. A lifetime would not be wasted at the bliss campground. Honestly, there is no wasted life. Even a life spent in the bowels of hell, deep in fear, riddled with the anxiety of separation is not wasted. It is a masterful training ground, a germination field ripe with the potential of harvest. Each moment embodied is grace, regardless of what it looks like.

My path always beckoned me further into the void of unknowing, and then a bit further yet. Stopping places flashed by in what seemed an endless stream of painful resistance and truth-altering shifts, the next five starting before the last ones finished. Curiosity killed the cat, they say ... and I am nothing if not curious.

The truth or the trappings—which do you want?

The first thing my earliest teacher told me was to be aware of the attraction that phenomena hold for us. He said that when I see clearly, I will notice it is all phenomena, a multiplicity of appearances. He was a pearl. I neither deserved nor earned his grace.

As I sat there listening, letting his words permeate, he said something to the effect of: *Do you want truth or the trappings?*

He was asking me to be clear about it, as certain as I could be if I truly wanted truth more than anything else. I used to wonder if he hadn't spoken those words to me with such force of love, if the search for truth, regardless of what it is, would have compelled me the way it did … or was it already deeply embedded in the inner blueprint?

Predestination … who wants to know?

That gets to the question: is life predestined? Is the script written from start to finish or does it slowly and creatively unfold with the revelation of each new experience? Are experiences just waiting to play their part? Are they lined up, awaiting their cue? Is it possible to know? Wouldn't knowing automatically create a knower, and by that very fact produce limited answers?

Does it matter? Who is it that cares? Is the appearance of choice, actually choice? How could it be when the inner blueprint, the karma and conditioning is running? Wouldn't the inner structures govern any choice?

Is awakening the choiceless abandonment of any need to know, and the letting-go of all beliefs one way or the other?

In a world of infinite possibilities could there be just one right way?

No one is unraveled the same way. Some want a different truth. There are as many truths as there are people. Some hearts soar surrounded by spiritual or religious trappings. Others may resonate with fame and fortune, or just the idea of being special. Some yearn to be called teacher. One is not better than the other. All paths are the path home. Some just include a few more roundabouts. The pull of the phenomenal is powerful and exciting, a stimulating draw. Life would be rather boring, not to mention unchanging, if everyone was alike.

There is nothing wrong with any version. All are pathways of experiencing. Most paths derive their sense of power from the outward-focused experience, the material world. Inexorably tied to the separation experience, the experience's imaginary plots and characters, they tender fleeting peace and happiness.

But not everyone is here for the infinite eternal experiential. Many are here experiencing the pull of the phenomenal, the delights of the chase. The informational field informs the seeking, offering opportunities to see how it feels to not find, and like steel striking rock and sparking fire, they are also fire starters for others' journeys, as are we all. The swirl of the totality is a master class of perpetual precision.

Could anything be different from what it is?

The interactive field is the heart of every experience. It is both giver and receiver, as is every expression, an infinity loop of creation and re-invention. Life's joys and apparent blessings, as well as falls from grace—the big, public ones of spiritual or religious teachers and secular leaders, to the less publicized, but no less felt, discord of everyday people—all are the effect of a causeless cause.

The activity of experiencing, of consciousness, alone *is*. It has never been about punishment or revenge, settling the score or doling out rewards—those are the separation story. The designless design, the improvisational jazz blowing the horn of life, simply unfolds as experience in perfect harmony with the aliveness-aligning, auto-correcting blueprint.

Since experience bends towards the recognition of what it is, it is impossible to maintain any solidification, finality, crystallization of delusion for long. Experience by its very beingness, its aliveness, exposes its core reality. The sheer effort it takes to resist the pull of the living dynamism, to resist the divine dance, the magic movement of *Infinite Aliveness*, to stay fixed in any seat, eventually precipitates a fall, the fall that points to a life lived outside the understanding of what life is.

Such efforts merely serve to expose the 'person' making the effort as a mental construct, the misidentified separate self. Nothing is stationary, not even the illusory constructs of an illusory mind, although for a short time they give an Oscar-worthy performance of changelessness. Actually, all is movement, all is the shimmer of abounding animation.

Are you ready to see?

The less crowded path, the path of what-the-heck-is-this-really is not as enticing. It certainly does not sell well. In separation's financially driven, money-focused world, it is easy to see why there is so little interest. Truthfully, few want to expose the fabrications of their lives. It requires an upending of the desire for peace and happiness, the need for fame and fortune, and the craving for acceptance and community.

You wouldn't consciously choose this.

That's where life's opportune push comes in.

All bets are off on the path of *Actuality*. Life itself eventually opens the door into the void, into not knowing, into the heart of uncertainty, into the valley of the shadow of death. Regardless of what you believe, there is no one who is not on the path. Sooner or later, the quest for truth appears. If not this moment, the next.

A collision course with delusion

The unknown terrifies … and there is truly nothing that can be known. You are not stripped of anything real, only the fallacies you hold dear.

Life is on a collision course with anything that is based in delusion, unstoppably unwinding the distortion until nothing of separation remains … and honestly, there is no way to know if it stops there. I tend to think not, but what do I know? That's not appealing to the assumed self. You can see why it does not sell. It's pretty hard to market that.

Wanting life as it is *not*, you remain focused on the imaginary pictures you are contriving, and cannot see past that story's star billing. Your vision quite literally stops at the boundary of believability your beliefs and desires have set. Blinded by the lights on the billboard, images of what's possible and what-needs-to-be gleaming in your eyes, you cannot see what is already here, standing right in front of you. There can be no thoughts of surrender. You cannot stop and go no further. Why would you? You'd have to be out of your mind to choose life as it is!

The separate self will never annihilate the separate self as much as it appears to try. Of yourself, you cannot surrender, cannot step off the cliff's edge into thin air, and yet, surrender occurs when you are readied, when you arrive at futility's scenic viewpoint, and can see the utter nonsense of placing your faith in what is not, the confounding, addictive experience of life's phenomenality.

When my teacher said *be aware of phenomena* it was a much bigger gift than I was capable of receiving. After hearing his words I poked around another twenty years, bloodying my forehead on dead ends, meeting the unavoidable—so many painful losses—until finally being humbled by life enough to open my eyes and heart, my belly and my soul, to what he was pointing at. I am not a slow learner but I like to say I am thorough (there's no obvious difference sometimes). Were another twenty years necessary? Maybe. All I can say is they were for me.

Experience, while not what it seems, and majestic beyond our capacity to conceive, is chock full of climbs to the top and falls into the depths. That is duality's nature. It is a land of birth and death, of ups and down, of light and dark. Right now, at our current stage in this 3D experiential, we are reaping what we have sown for years, having sown from anger and fear, having taken this alive beauty and turned it into dead matter.

A time of quickening

We are experiencing a quickening, deaths beyond numbers, a legion of falls and what seems like swiftly approaching darkness. Experience cannot but show us the blood and guts in which we placed our faith, mankind's ills arising out of ignorance, the natural aftereffect of not knowing who we are, what we are.

It seems that we, the peoples of earth, are unknowingly rewriting the collective bargaining agreement, and renegotiating the price to stay and play here on this amazing blue ball. We are far beyond solutions that come out of the old-world mindset of fear and force, intimidation and threats, the stuff of separation. That approach has borne rotten fruit.

The bar is lifting, and collectively we are that which is placing it on ever higher supports.

Experience viewed from the separate self is incapable of inclusion and compassion, of consideration for that which is outside of self-interest. Love, peace, and harmony are not its nature. We either remember who we are, awaken wholesale from the belief in two, or eventually this shared existential experiment will implode.

And even that would not be a life-ender, just an earth-ender, the natural consequence of fear-based living. The tipping point has never been fixed. It is perpetually renewable, despite the appearance of earth's rapidly approaching end. The same goes for the objects we call humans.

To live a human life without knowledge of your beauty is beyond hard, an achingly sad substitute. It foretells a death sentence, a forced march into hell and heaven, a tug-of-war between the angels and the devils of your own making. It is also a grand ride, generally when viewed after the fact and when the fight or flight response peters out—whew!

Incarnation—why bother?

From the view of separation, experience is inebriating, attractive. It offers infinite possibilities, unending turns on the Ferris wheel of fate. Lifetime after lifetime, you joyously slide back into bodies for another go. There is a reason you incarnate. As my mother said from the other side just before another turn: *It all looks great from here.* It is only once you arrive, when you find your infinite self in a finite body, once the expansiveness contracts and conforms that the primal scream, the one only you can hear, the one that does not utter a peep, begins to seep out of your soul.

Thankfully, this isn't a material world. It looks like one, feels like one, seems like one, but it is made of consciousness, not matter as commonly believed, and therefore is spontaneously responsive to changes in consciousness.

Years ago, I was given a vision:

> I saw a woman with a long white braid walking toward a polluted river. Eyes brimming with tears, she bent down on one knee to embrace the earth. I could feel love emanating from her. She leaned over and one single tear fell into the stagnant water. Within minutes the river cleared. The fish came to life. The entire eco-system breathed anew. The tear was pure love, unconditional essence distilled into a salty drop. This manifestation, this holographic world, responds powerfully to love. Nothing is ever beyond its reach.

So why bother? Why take the path less traveled? There really is no reason. Life does not need a reason, and it is not a reasonable choice you make anyway. Life simply takes you where it will. One day, having walked far enough down the path of phenomenality, you turn and surprisingly find yourself three steps down the path of truth and wisdom, knowing that anything short of recognizing what is real will never satisfy the craving within.

To live a human life with the knowledge of what you are, rather than being a death sentence, is a sentence of aliveness, a mad funhouse experiential, an endless compassionate playground manifesting out of, in, and as, all-encompassing experiencing.

Directly experiencing what you truly are shifts malevolence to benevolence, exclusion to inclusion, the disparate warring parts to the compassionate whole.

If the choice was yours, that by itself is a good enough reason to bother.

CHAPTER 6

Experiencing

What is experience?

Has it any substantiality, any stability? The fact that you are experiencing is quite clear. Can you deny it? Is it not always changing, appearing, and disappearing in unceasing motion? Can you pin it down? Many have tried and failed.

Can you catch smoke from a fire? It may drive you crazy, leave its smell in your clothing. It may even cause you to get up and move, but catch it you cannot. It slips right through your fingers, a will-o'-the-wisp, never taking on the same appearance from one second to the next.

That's experience.

Experience is not malleable. There must be something to mold, to shape, to hold, for it to be malleable. Is there anything to grasp? To conquer? When nothing lasts, when whatever appears doesn't hang around, what's left? Experience is constantly overcoming, reinventing, reimagining itself. What's here one moment simply disappears in the next.

Can you see the inherent freedom?

How do you respond to the uncertainty, the absolute impermanence of the only bit of veneer you can somewhat verify—your own experience? Do you see the freedom inherent in that insubstantiality, or do you force it into a conceptual box and plaster it with labels: *time, space, subject, object, world*? Nothing that can be labeled exists the way you think, and that pretty much covers all experience.

It is more feasible to say what experience is not than what it is, and even that will trip you up.

Experience is constantly changing, a flow of vital aliveness experienceable as perception, sensation, thought and emotion. It is a dynamic field of Actuality, of Presence, of *This That Is*. That which is present, experiencing itself, is the field of knowing that is inseparable from all things known; conscious awareness aware of itself; this Infinite Aliveness. Experiencing never changes, only the contents appear, morph, or disappear, and they too are This, are What Is, just not in the way you presume.

Snips and snails and puppy dog tails

What is experience made of? Does it come from somewhere? Does it check out now and then? If so, where does it go?

Is there awareness and experiencing?

Awareness looks through your eyes, yes, but it also experiences the body's sensations. Is it not special and sacred while being quite ordinary and commonplace? Look for yourself.

Who or what is experiencing your experience?

Ask yourself that question and fall into the answer. It may

feel like a stepping back, a dropping in. Explore that awareness, the experiencing.

Where do *you* stop and *I* begin?

Are there really two, yours and another's? Can you find a seam where you stop, and the other begins? Is it possible that the exact same awareness experiences through all portals of experiencing?

Probe your experience.

It is not what you think.

Can you let your presumptions drop for a few minutes? There's no harm in that, or is there? When you were a baby, you didn't have labels for anything—not your hands, your body, your mother, not anything. Allow yourself to be that innocent, that stripped of everything known, and be simple. Simply experience what is here now without naming anything, without determining what is happening, without needing to know what is here or what you are.

If there isn't a storyline are *you* still present?

What is present without your labels, without: birth, hands and legs, body and mind, chair, floor and roof, self and others, sky and world, dimensions and death? What is sensation without naming it painful, intense, sensual, or gentle?

As the labels slip into obscurity, your grip on what you *think* is here gradually adjusts so that you can see what is *really* here. One experience at a time, life fine-tunes your hold on it until your hands fall open—they have nothing left to hang onto. Allowing yourself to look, to experience life without labels is part of the extrication.

Allow yourself to feel your experience without any label. You *are* the feeling, the experiencing. When you stay here without moving you realize that there is nothing but experiencing, not the experiencing of, but fundamental experiencing. It is the bottom floor of knowing, for all objects appear out of the field of experiencing, including you.

When the burdens of knowledge collapse on the ground what remains? You. You do. You call that remainder, I.

What is that *I*, the one who experiences life?

Drop your pat answers if you can. Stop a moment and see for yourself. Without your presumptions and theories what do you know for sure? What is left?

Take your time.

Is there anything you can experience—anything in life—anything at all that is separate from basic experiencing, anything that can be experienced without you?

This is not a mental exercise, it's not just about reasoned thinking. *Feel* into it. Experience the answer.

Are you not the given in all life's equations?

Just maybe, you are not what you thought.

How can you say what the world is if you do not understand the lens through which you know? Until you realize what experiencing is, what sight and sound, sensation and emotion are made of, what thought is and where it comes from, how can you truly know anything? Stopping to investigate, making first contact with your experience, no different than diving into the ocean to understand what ocean is, you see that life is not what you thought.

Does your body appear in a world, or do body and world

appear in experiencing?

What is the lens through which the world is known?

Does not all that you know or could know, all that you can verify—no hearsay here—appear as experiencing?

Is there a you and an experiencing?

Dive in and see, and it quickly becomes self-evident that what you call two is not *two* at all but inseparable *Infinite Aliveness*.

Experiencing—get out of your head and into your life

Stop. Open. Feel. Experience. There is nothing more important in life.

The nature of experience is equally as important as the gold standard inquiry of who you are. Both take you to the recognition that consciousness experiences itself through, and as, separate expressions that are nothing other than itself. It's a pretty cool mirage, and still not the sum total of what you are for you are the nifty appearance of self, the whole world, the universe in its entirety, and every imaginable dimension. You, my dear one, rock.

You go nowhere without experiencing. Where you go, it goes. See a pattern? Experiencing is so basic, so profoundly simple, it is completely overlooked.

Wherever you place your focus, life pops into being. There is no end to your creativity. If you look through the most powerful telescope available, you will always experience something, even if it is you experiencing what appears to be nothing. You are *Infinite Aliveness* experiencing this thing called life and all its supposedly separate expressions and experiences. This wondrous human creature that you think of as me is *Infinite Aliveness* in drag.

It is not nothing—it's infinity at play

Just because life is not what you thought, it doesn't mean it is nothing. It is consciously aware experiencing, and it is everything. You do not exist as you thought. So what? That is great news. That calls for celebration. Experiencing is all there is, that is, if *is* isn't taken too seriously, too solidly.

As you sink deeper into the field you notice what experiencing really is, the shimmering light, the tingling buzz, the infinite field at play.

Experiencing doesn't end with your body, doesn't cease when your body dies. The body arises in experiencing. Experiencing does not arise within or outside a body as our culture believes.

Don't believe me. Don't believe your mind's old program. Look and see. When you look with empty curiosity it is self-evident, a verifiable surprise and not at all what you thought.

Fallacies abounding

You, like every human on the planet, were brainwashed. The world of separation is awash with misinformation, the biggest piece being the idea that you are a physical body in a physical world. That idea is the beginning and end of you. You were pointed away from your direct experience to the objects within it, to the resistance code, the improvement game, to the unworthiness supposedly embedded in your very nature.

Whether you were raised with Christianity or not, the idea of original sin, that you were born flawed, is in play throughout the world. You are influenced by it whether it's personal to you or not.

Marketing schemes, politicians, those who want to exert control, capitalize on the flaw. A woman's place in society is marked by it. The way you view others as people to be feared has the flaw at its foundation. When you do something harmful you were taught to say: *It is human nature to do bad things*, or: *What can I say; it's who I am*. Only the masters, the brilliant few, the rare beings should, let alone can live a life of a saint, right? The fact that you recognize saints, the special individuals who overcame or ascended, rather than the truth of what we all are, points to the misinformation you have been fed.

You have never needed to be saved

Seeing this is the invitation to turn around, to turn and face, to feel your intimate, palpable, sensual immediate experience and watch as the carefully crafted brainwashed folly washes away.

> You were never lost and alone, unworthy, or in need of saving.

The truth of who you are has always been right in front of you. You were not abandoned. That could never be. Impossible, it is. You have never been untended and have not made one single mistake. No one has. What a relief!

Hidden—well, not exactly—within experience is that to which all teachings point. It only feels hidden because you think you know what experience is.

What if you don't?

Intrinsic to all experience is its reality, what it really is, what this is, what you are. Experience is the precious pearl, the alpha and omega pointer. That is the true miracle of a human incarnation. Regardless of the contents of experience, whether they impart joy or sadness, grief or sorrow, finding out what experiencing really is, what this is, is possible through your messed-up exquisitely precious human experience.

A human life is better than a winning lottery ticket, and the odds are 100% in your favor when you are simply willing to stop and meet it truly, deeply and innocently.

CHAPTER 7

Thoughts Do Not Think

You have a brain, and it houses a mind that tells you what to think, what to believe. That's the story the materialist world tells. You are a body, and the body has within it a mind. Consciousness, they say, also lives within the body. That is the tale, but is it accurate?

What you call your mind is a compilation of thoughts, thoughts piled one upon another, not a mind thinking, but thoughts.

Thoughts do not think, and the brain, an appearance in the mirage of life, if assigned a function, would be a processor—not a thinker.

If that is true, what does that mean for thinking, and where does that leave you?

Thoughts lined up like little ducks in a row, a trick of life appearing to be embedded in the spacetime continuum, make thoughts appear to be thinking. When you look closely, emptied of your preconceptions, you will comprehend that thoughts do not think. That fact is not hidden. It is quite obvious if you are willing to concede a little of what you know.

One thought at a time? Not so!

Thoughts are not contiguous. They don't hold hands in a queue. If they are joined at all, it is by the gaps between them. Their only semblance of continuity is assigned by yet another thought.

Were they not placed like diamonds in the golden setting of consciousness you would easily perceive thoughts for what they are: little blips of energy arising in and disappearing instantly, dissolving back into consciousness.

Were it not for consciousness, there would be no continuity. Aliveness, disguised as you, lends thoughts the continuity of beingness. The sense that they belong to you, that they mean something, are more thoughts, thoughts not flowing out of the separate self, but the *Infinite Aliveness* you are. The sense of ownership is very natural, and accurate since everything belongs to you, to this pure experiencing you are. There is nothing that is not you.

A thought pops into conscious awareness and vanishes. Can you separate the thought from awareness or is there simple awareness aware of a thought? Are there two, a thought and awareness?

Don't let double vision fool you

What is true on one level is true on all levels, or it is not true at all. Doubles, and triples, and more, seem to be everywhere, all the time, any way you look, and because they are, you get to playfully joyfully woefully experience the many exquisite appearances of twoness, even though there is no such thing as two. Double vision is quite the trickster. If you were one of many, an actual factual *you* who owned her or his thoughts, if subject and object were verifiably real, stand-alone pieces of the human puzzle, wouldn't you be able to control which thoughts appear?

They would be yours to summon or dismiss, but it's obvious that they are not. You do not control which thoughts appear or how long they hang around. You say you have a body, that it is yours and yet, you cannot control it. If separate selves had power, we would all be healthy, slim, trim, exquisitely beautiful specimens of humanity.

Mind, body, and thought are objects in awareness, appearances in experiencing.

Bodies do what they do. Thoughts arise and fall as they do. There seems to be a magnetic pool of resonance, a delineated data field making up the specifics of each human's experience, but it is not self-contained, nor static. It is permeable, without lines of demarcation, and undergoing continuous change. The field changes as experiencing adds to it. Experience—life—changes you, changes me, altering and expanding the ever-changing infinite possibilities of its expression.

Eventually the dam must break ... aren't you tired of holding it together?

Trying to make life lie down and roll over on command doesn't work. Attempting to make life conform, express itself as you want it to, hurry up or slow down, is akin to making it play dead. It might give the appearance for a moment or two but hang on a bit and resurrect itself it will. Just like a thought, you can suppress it for a while, but anything suppressed bounces back vigorously.

Suppression—decompression—resistance—surrender—it is all part of the experiencing.

Suppression is not necessarily wrong, nor is surrender necessarily right. Thoughts, contrary to collective assumption, need not be controlled—it's not possible to control them.

A thought arises followed by the thought, *I like*, or *I don't like this thought*. A grand attempt at suppression, or conversely, ways to stimulate its manifestation, ensues. There is no original thought, no thought that you think. No separate self has ever had an original thought, a thought that belongs to it.

Granted, it does seem that some thoughts trigger more thinking, building castles, expanding universes on the backs of the ones that came before, sowing new thoughts one after the other, like corn seeds in freshly tilled earth, a thought garden of inspiration or desolation. Look more closely if you will. What is the experience called thought? What is thought's reality?

Don't believe a word I write ... find out for yourself

Sense into one singular thought, any thought. (It doesn't matter what the thought seems to be saying.) Focus and feel. What does this one thought feel like? What is it made of? Is there a thread linking thought to thought ... or not?

Are there two—thought and experience, or experience and experiencer? Are you not the seed, the garden, and the farmer ... the thought, the apparent thinking, and the movement after? Look with free and uncluttered eyes, empty of anything but the seeing, and you will find that it can't be divided up.

When you stop and directly experience the mental chatter you see that thought appears. Its appearance may seem to trigger another thought, a physical sensation, or a mental perception. All the triggered reactions are experiences arising in awareness, just like the thought.

Awareness—simple experiencing—is the constancy, the backdrop and foreground, not to mention the stuff that makes up all the apparent responses.

Is there anything else that you can find for certain?
Isn't it interesting that you can find the insubstantiality, but you cannot truly name it, cannot know it.
Ah ... a pointer in an ocean of pointers.

Empty space isn't empty

Consciousness, awareness, experiencing—is the glue, the apparent linkage of thoughts and responses, making thoughts seem to be thinking, denoting the passage of time, validating a separate self and a world.

The infinite cannot know anything without the finite experience. Knowing is the finite experience. Thought is one aspect of that experience. As infinity, there is nothing to know. Without the appearance of a separate world there is nothing to experience and no one to experience it. That does not mean it is a physical world, in the way that we usually think of it, any more than the dreams that feel real, that you experience as real, are materially real.

The idea that I am separate is a thought too. Just because

the thought: *I am this body-mind* arises, does that make it so? No. Of course, not. What you believe yourself to be is nothing but a string of thoughts: *I am me. I am my history. I am changing. I am in pain. I am ascending. I am awake. I am separate. I am human. I will die.* It is all thought, thoughts that come and go, that arise and fall, disappearing back into that from which they come.

Simply notice

When you notice your thoughts, following them as they come and go, attending to them, feeling into them, you see that they are phantasms, imagination, apparitions in the catacombs of conditioning, having not one whit of substantiality other than as precious dream enchantments, the experience called thought.

You do not create with your thoughts and their natural fallout—beliefs. You perceive life with them. They season awareness with your favorite flavors, the spices of your life. Thoughts arise, not *your* thoughts, but basic unowned thoughts, conjuring up a banquet of perception and sensation.

Beliefs are equally flimsy for they are a collection of thoughts.

What we see, our perceptions, are our interpretation of light and shadow, color and textures filtered through thoughts.

It's all mind, but not mind the way it is commonly perceived.

You are not doing the thinking; aliveness is thinking *you*.

As thoughts dissolve, what you see changes. Thoughts cannot be dissolved with insistence and resistance, with any attempt to change them. Fighting them gives them strength, makes them more real to you, for you do not need to fight with illusions. You fight what you believe to have reality.

When thoughts are seen for what they are, unsubstantiated, lacking ground upon which to stand, they fall apart without needing to do anything. The very doing, the resistance, maintains, sustains and entrains the fantasy.

The idea that there is something to overcome is a thought; the idea that enlightenment is possible, a thought; the concept of separation, a thought; the idea that you should be able to control your thoughts, a thought; the hope for escape, a thought.

See what thoughts are and there's nothing to overcome.

CHAPTER 8

Cause and Effect

Cause is an interesting word, as words go. The belief in cause is present when you are scampering around trying to figure it all out, when you are attempting to alleviate the pain. You may tell yourself that if you can get to that root cause you will be able to fix or repair your life, or at the very least, head off another disaster of the same kind.

Cause, according to the bag of thoughts you call 'mind', is the source of all problems, the home address of blame. Whoever, whatever, caused the breach in happiness, the ruptured peace, must be named. When tracked down, when pinpointed with precision, you think it will finally deliver you from the sensation of walking blindfolded along the edge of a thousand-foot drop. If you find your way to that source, life will feel less precarious, less blind, so you feel that your mission is to find the cause and seize control.

Cause: the polluters of purity; politicians who defy reason; family members who don't love adequately; genetics, bacteria, the fount of illness; all the reasons happiness eludes you; the spoilers of life. The list is endless. This world is based on assigning cause, on judgment and blame. When life is not the way it is 'supposed' to be, when it doesn't dance to the tune of your opinion, or accord with powerful enough group's agenda, the scapegoat is sacrificed, bled out, not a lot different from human sacrifices of yore.

Finding the 'true cause' is the ultimate game of hide-and-seek

There's but one hitch. Cause—true cause—that illusive, elusive phantom cannot be definitively found no matter how hard you look, unless you want to blame life itself. When you are willing to let that in you'll see that it pinpoints something of inestimable value.

Cause and *why* are a fine example of co-dependency. *Why* is the biggest small word in the dictionary, replete with an unending supply of possible definitions, the least of which—also the closest to truth as we can get in words—is the answer to cause's conundrum: *for no reason at all.*

Yikes! Can I have a different answer?

You don't like that one. Most humans don't. We tend to rail against it without considering its accuracy. If there really is no reason, no answer to *why,* then the probability of no cause skyrockets, and if there is no cause then, bloody hell, that means you are stuck with life as it is—until it changes on its own, which you inconveniently forget it is always doing.

So, you continue to ask why, to try and find the cause, the cause of lack, the reason for your sadness, the bottom of the well of grief, the damnable seed of your unhappiness, not realizing that your search for a golden goose, a goose that will alter cause's effect, creates the experience of a disappointing life in the first place.

When you can't find a reason for your dismay, the next

natural step is to blame, to lay your unhappiness at the door of the mean and nasty, uncaring and unfeeling *other*, spreading vitriol as you project your pain, breaking your heart into ever smaller pieces. By 'heart' I don't mean the organ beating inside your chest. I am pointing at the heart of experiencing. It is the sacred heart of awareness, the one heart, the love that fuels the universe. Blame tears you apart, casting off the split-apart pieces of your own self, making you feel less and less whole, intensifying the pain.

Blaming—it's primal!

The alternative is to stop and experience life as it is, directly without the buffer of blame—but that is more than most of us can allow. We are so enwombed in the blame game that we cannot see any other possibility when faced with pain and suffering, discomfort and failure ... basically not getting what we want. Blame is the automatic default; it's a primal survival instinct.

Blame, even self-blame, is a finger pointing to something other, a cure or cause assigned to the pain, a scapegoat to summon a safe space, a wall between you and your immediate experience.

Blame arises in the space of shielded awareness, wherein the bud is still too tender to open from its slumber. It has not yet developed sufficient trust, the requisite resilience to thrive outside of its tight confines.

Within the bud you don't stop and consider that maybe there is no reason, that life is just the way it is, that it is filled with happiness and sadness, grief and joy, peace and irritation, and seeing that, let it be. To one tightly wrapped in what *should be* that is inconceivable, unthinkable.

Avoidance tactics—have they ever changed *What Is?*

Life is what it is and there truly isn't anyone to blame, nor is there a safe space to be found. Blame simply delays the inevitable discovery, for as the bud reaches ample ripeness, as life's sun and rain impart what is needed for growth, the recognition cannot but take place. Life shows you what you've been doing, how you have blamed and laid cause at any door in order to not feel, to avoid experiencing the pain that you were sure you could not let in, and your default begins to shift.

You see that you do not understand your unhappiness and you won't, until you stop and allow yourself to feel what you feel, to experience your life as it is, to meet what is actually here. You realize that avoidance, in its many forms, has kept you at arm's length from your life and you honestly do not know what it is. All that you know is the story you have been telling yourself about it.

The view is clearer now, but still seen through a glass darkly. It's just not as dark as before. The backdrop of light is peeking through. You are not the cause of your misery, but as you open your eyes and meet your life, it may seem like you were always the problem. That is a misunderstanding of what is real, not unlike the idea that avoidance protects you. Self-blame is blame *redirection*, not blame *eradication*. That fallacy clears up as you tread further down the path.

'No cause'—a scary idea?

Seeing cause more clearly is a powerful step. You notice that not having to assign blame feels good.

Unresisted life doesn't hurt quite so much; wanting life to fit your image of what is right and good intensifies the pain.

You see that your resistance pushes those who love you away. It was you who refused them access to your breaking heart and penned the story you used to blame them for not showing up.

In that very limited sense you are the cause ... and yet, you are not. Your patterns and models, the beliefs that form your inner ruts, cannot be other than they are until they have been seen for what they are. The seeing releases them. True seeing, seeing the absolute futility of hanging onto them, is the releasing. It is not something you do, but something that occurs as the support struts, the foundational thoughts for the beliefs, crumble.

That is what life is—the crumbling of all that you hold sacrosanct, the shattering of the precious inner idols, the expansion of the contractions, the great return.

What if you are staging your own reality show?

There is no cause. What you experience as life is the causelessness of life life-ing, of God God-ing, *Infinite Aliveness* expressing. It is not personal, so very not personal, even though it feels utterly personal. Life is a super-intense reality show, but it's just not real in the way real is usually defined.

Why is one person's inner landscape filled with boulders, and another's nothing but flat rocks? There's that word again—*why?* The question assumes a self and others, a cause and effect that is personal. There is not-two, although there is the appearance and the experience of *two*, of me and you and the world. That's a big fly in the ointment from a human point of view. It is a convincing appearance, but be that as it may, it is still *Infinite Aliveness* creating, engendering something out of nothing, a rabbit popping out of infinity's hat.

Who is to blame for all this? No one!

There is no one to blame. There is no one, period. Life does what it does. It appears to strike one of its expressions down and lift another up. That is the experience, the illusion, but it is not the truth of you.

Cause and effect are but the tip of misdirection. There are so many falsehoods you take to be true, and so much that is true that you are certain is false. When the pain reaches the perfect temperature, the misinterpretation bubbles to the top and pops open to plead its case: I am innocent. I was never what you thought.

By now you suspect that all this is life itself, so:

There can be no one to blame.
How would life blame its own expression?

CHAPTER 9

Not Knowing

Beginner's mind, a world of uncertainty, students forever ... not at all what the separate self wants to hear. It wants answers and certainty; it wants to graduate from the pain and suffering; it wants to be okay. Not knowing the answers, being uncertain, are the hallmarks of losers, right?

Life here is tough. These physical bodies all have death sentences hanging over them. You get to keep nothing, and even worse, you will lose everything and everyone you love ... or so it goes. As the separate self, you stand upon a foundation of shifting sand. Like the sand in an hourglass, it empties itself out, diminishing your allocation of days. It is natural to want to know. Knowing feels like it adds several degrees of safety, layers of highly sought protection. Perhaps if you see it coming, if you know what's out there, you can take a detour and not crash head-on into the unknown.

Do you think knowing will save you?

If you stop a moment and allow yourself to feel into that reality, to accept the death sentence, to walk up the steps to the (figurative) gallows and let the rope tighten around your neck, you get a small sense of the anxiety and fear you carry, and reflexively deny, chiefly without a scrap of real evidence.

Your denial is of the separate self's finish line, the last arrival, the final departure, the escape clause you so desperately seek while inwardly knowing there's no chance to save the day. Not one of us will avoid the experience called death ... and such is the plight of the human residing in separation, the one who was born and will die, who is curled up in the corner screaming to be heard, to be saved, to be real.

What makes you think you need to be saved?

This *you are* has no finish line, no arrival point, no one to be done, no one to overcome, transcend or ascend. No one is a teacher, no one a student. There is but one singularity, the one without another ... and there is the precious miraculous arising of singular expressions, this awareness endlessly unfolding expanding contracting as innocent new appearances.

Convinced you are separate, you skip right past the evidence perfectly primed to demonstrate the truth. In your rush to give permanence to an ephemeral character—for the separate self is nothing but the dream of personal sovereignty cloaked in audacity, the blasphemy which divides and subtracts, detaches and detracts—you cut the singularity, the one that is not-two into pieces and claim your exclusive kingdom on earth.

> The infinite intelligence within you knows that your dream of self is not substantial.

It knows that it is indeed a dream you will never awaken to as real, but you go through the motions anyway. To give it up feels impossible, so contrary and utterly destructive to what you know.

We humans are silly creatures, painfully so.

As soon as you know anything ...

Knowing anything at all limits the expression, binds what is experienced to what is merely known. That is not something you need years of study to understand. It's obvious if you pay the slightest bit of attention and are willing to risk finding out. It is the reason eyewitnesses are notoriously wrong. Nearly all humans see through the lens of what we believe is true and miss what is actually here.

Experiencing isn't altered by knowing, but our experience of it is. Knowing maintains the focus on what is separate, rather than what is present. Life's an optical illusion, and through it you are conditioned to see separation where none exists. Diving into the naked experience, perception shifts. The ten thousand separate things stand down, revealed for what they actually are. They are what they have always been—simple basic magical miraculous experiencing, experiencing without an experiencer.

Our conditioning automatically assumes an experiencer because—to our separate self—the truth of the matter seems to be too insane to consider. The experience of a lifetime is not simply the precious gift of the lifetime itself but eternal experience, *Infinite Aliveness*. When life stops you, opening your eyes to what is here, all ideas of self and other, the normally accepted faith in separation, disintegrates.

Certainty is not the antidote ... it's the toxin itself

Any understanding that preserves a knower is separation. Holding on to even a smidgen of the need to know creates the very situation that you ache to escape. There are myriad attractive escape routes for a wily escape artist, but from the space of tightly held beliefs there is no escape. Beliefs make up a cage and the knowing that comes from beliefs creates the hamster's cell, putting the wheel and carrot in place. It's all round and round, uphill and down from there. You're on that wheel, riding, sliding the slippery slope into pain and suffering, with little flashes of light, tastes of love, glimmers of hope, glimpses of freedom: just enough to steady you on your great escape, to give the appearance of getting somewhere.

The wheel spins, just fast enough to maintain the hope-filled display of beliefs that got you onto the wheel. You won't see anything but what you believe until you are ready to believe your eyes might be deceiving you.

You put yourself in the hamster cage and throw away the key, blocking the exit with unassailable certainty. Pain is a dandy motivator. In the attempt to avoid pain, real pain, deep core pain, we humans will do most anything. We will even inflict pain on ourselves.

Life itself is your mirror

Fortunately, life shows you what you are doing. When you look with fresh eyes, unshaded by beliefs, you can see it. What you see—the outer expression—demonstrates your state of alignment with what actually is. It cannot not. That's its thing. Your world—yes, each person lives in their own world—is a holographic display of the precisely detailed blueprint. Manifestation changes as the data field informing the blueprint shifts, complete with a little lag time. Pain is the clarion call, the dharma bell saying pay attention, there's something here that wants to be seen.

The inner cannot help but be changed by every new

experience, every sight that is seen, noted or not, every bell that rings, every song that plays, every taste exploding in your mouth, even the tiniest touch, skin on skin, or a simple pat on the shoulder of a thick, fluffy jacket. With each bit of new data the build is altered—sometimes exponentially, sometimes incrementally and often seemingly not at all.

You are the resurrection

A resurrection is always taking place, resurrecting the old, creating the new. This resurrection is life, normal everyday human experience.

If you could see what experience actually is, if you could be open to the possibility that you do not know, could not know, then the outer expression of life would change instantly, but that's not the way it generally happens. It seems to take a bit more repetition, a shaking quaking ripping stripping of the old to unsettle the beliefs, the conditioning that has settled in.

Willingness—the willingness to be proven wrong comes first, and it flows out of your hard-earned experience, from hints of possibility peeking through the shadows, creeping into the static beliefs and closed heart. Willingness is the crack that fills with ice and weakens the bedrock, beginning the grand reveal of separation's distortion. Once that first crack appears, more are sure to follow. Earthquakes and landslides, massive volcanic eruptions, typhoons and 500-mile-wide hurricanes, aren't even in the same class as this disruption.

Where does it go from there, from that first crack?

Into the heart of not-knowing, the recognition that you simply cannot know what this is, that this is beyond words.

ACTUALITY

Trying to string words together, to convey what reality is may happen, may even be fun, but ultimately will get you nowhere.

Eventually you discover that nowhere is a great place to hang out and just *be*.

CHAPTER 10

Patience ... Wait for It

With your willingness—and if you are reading this book that bridge has been crossed—a crack has opened in your carefully constructed sense of self. Now, instead of the righteously protected separate self, the guard dog has a little longer run-out chain. You are willing, but everything doesn't automatically change, and when it does change it may not be in the way you wanted.

Our wants, desires and self-defined needs are the territory of the separate self, of the mistaken view.

This *That Is* would never fill your life with proof of what it is not, with evidence to bolster separation.

Surrender isn't a bargain to get a better life

You cannot surrender what you know and expect life to magically give you what you want. That is not true surrender, is it? That's playing a game with life, the sense of separation feigning willingness in order to get what it desires. That is manipulation, not surrender.

You cannot know what will manifest in your life. Old

karma will play out, possibly lifetimes of old karma, not only personal karma but collective karma too. Bear in mind, the one is not-two. The beauty of not knowing, of being willing to not know, is it eases the transition from life as a never-ending karma machine, to one that begins to clear the slate.

Needing to know is an attempt to manipulate the flow

Manifestation is like a pipeline filled with oil and water. Upstream the shift to willingness enters the flow, even though downstream the pipeline is still full of what came before, dense sticky oil, the natural outcomes of fear and anxiety, unwillingness and inflexibility. As willingness enters the pipeline, the possibility of not knowing appears, and a flow of love, the acceptance of experience as it is, adds to the mix, the mix that is not just yours personally. That doesn't necessarily mean that difficult events disappear from life. Some may; some may not. There's no way to know, but your experience of the events begins to shift.

Metaphors such as pipelines are as close to the mystery as words can go. Whether the extrapolation from experience to words is accurate or not is debatable, for nothing is knowable, controllable, or certain. Life is constantly evolving, expanding. What feels accurate today is absorbed and expanded upon, creating the foundation from which the next tidbit of truth, the next reality reveal takes center stage.

Can you find a time when you chose your thoughts, beliefs or experiences?

What's interesting is that you don't control what is added to the flow. It seems like you choose to let go, to open yourself to new possibilities, but you didn't choose the experiences that brought you to the point that looked like a decision. You do not control the inflow. Life gives you, the apparent human, experiences that feel like choice, that feel like being human, without one bit of real harm. How could the unborn, never dying, be harmed? It's a stupendous arrangement that is without need or judgment.

As the pipeline empties, as life is lived by surprise in refined acceptance, curious to explore the next appearance, the dense oily contents begin to flow more like water, a surge of life as it is. If there are hidden reservoirs of resistance—and there probably will be—those are flushed out too, just like they've always been, only now you are more open to seeing them, more willing to be shown. It's less scary, less painful. Life now affords a loftier—wider view—experience. Even with the broader scope, you still won't know what's coming. You might get hints, but there is no way to truly know.

While you resonate with the separate self who wants life his way, you will encounter disappointment.

When you come to the grace of not minding what appears, life shifts again. Does it get better? Does the manifestation improve? Not exactly. You just don't mind what appears.

Sometimes it's what the old you would call 'good,' sometimes not.

Dance, baby, dance!

Don't expect it to be magical—it won't be, unless you don a magician's cape, practicing wish-craft, experimenting with control in the zone of separation, rather than free-dancing with this, which is infinitely uncontrollable. That too is *This That Is*, the experiencing, the everything and nothing, all things and no things. It just won't offer the experience of lasting peace and happiness, for it has within it the fully-fledged seed of separation, and as is the nature of the sinfully precious, severed experience, that seed must sprout and be harvested.

Not only may it not be magical, peaceful and happy—it very likely won't be easy. Indeed, it may be excruciating at times, so much so that you'll wonder what the hell you were thinking, but there is no going back. You cannot uncrack that which is splitting asunder. You cannot see that you were unwilling without willingness, and you have seen. You cannot take a blackout pill and wipe out what is now real to you. A glimmer of truth would still shine in the heart of oblivion.

You've seen into the maze and it's not what you were told. You are active within the dream, within the sense of separation, even though the dream still seems like the old reality most of the time. You have yet to meet the truth of experiencing, what is, what is not.

Life is painful. There's no way around it. Life is filled with uncontrollable, unexplainable pain.

A few years back, for no reason at all, my heart went into ventricular tachycardia with no warning. I was walking to the recycle bin with a piece of cardboard and life changed. I went from a picture of health to being unable to stand in the blink of an eye.

If that wasn't enough of an in my face, you aren't in control moment, in the hospital while they figured out they couldn't figure it out, my body began shocking me, little shocks and big ones, quick ones and some that ran from my toes to my head … and none of the doctors would take it seriously which felt like a blistering slap on top of the discombobulating pain.

I couldn't fall asleep because the shocks occurred just as I was dropping off ... mostly. They were unnerving and filled me with a sense of dread, so much so that I held my breath each time fearing the shock would trigger my heart's malfunction. The worst of it lasted several months and kept me on pins and needles awaiting the final shock, the one that would end it all.

Nothing I did helped, and I tried everything. I did a deep dive into any article I could find, added extra pillows, slept with no pillows, adjusted my body position, prayed with reverence and screamed at God's cruelty. Then one night, totally exhausted, I finally gave up. I lay in bed and let the shocks come as they would. They were coming anyway, so I let them be, accepting that I might never sleep again, that I might live with the pain and uncertainty for the rest of my life, or that I might get lucky and die.

The last option felt like a winner at the time. Death sounded pretty damn good. Maybe I had to reach the point where I didn't care if I lived or died. I don't know. All I know is that I quit resisting the shocks ... and miraculously, that night at least, I slept, not because I had a wonderful spiritual epiphany, but because I had nothing left to fight with. Life was stripping the fight out of me, and rather than being a curse, it was a blessing.

Life is painful, and it is even more painful when we resist.

Without resistance even physical pain shifts its intensity, still painful but more manageable.

Resistance, the separate self, is the dreamer of pain. The

sense of separation is the aversion to *What Is*, the need to understand, the desire to make it better, the very natural wants and needs of the fictitious human. It is the dream of pain and joy, sadness and happiness, war and peace.

It's always been in your blood

True human beingness draws you forward, compels you to continue, even though you don't quite understand what is tugging at you. The thirst to see, to know what is actually true, is in your blood. It was always in your blood. It is the nature of your nature, and like cells reproducing by mitosis, the drive intensifies, growing with each new experience. It is silently, ever more swiftly consuming you. In the beginning the growth seems miniscule but it is picking up speed, compounding.

So, wait for it! Patience isn't something we humans are known for. In this world, making haste is perceived as better than taking your time. Such an ingrained perception goes with you on the spiritual path, so you can't understand why seeing through the fabrication takes so long.

A seed germinates, cracking open as it readies to reach through the dirt to the sky. Willingness is the germination stage. Everything that came before, the entirety of your life to that point, was not living. It was a shell game. Many of us are embodied but never break free of the shell. Some seeds don't sprout.

Prior to the advent of willingness, your seed was still snuggled inside the airless, airtight packet waiting to be sown. You have only begun to live. Patience is your friend and life can't help but create the circumstances for you to get to know each other better. Being in a hurry isn't faster. This is a journey to nowhere.

A kindergarten simulation

Perhaps we are the true human equivalents of pre-schoolers in a kindergarten simulation begining the journey of transformation. That feels accurate to me, this true human youngster. Wouldn't that be fun? Just think of all there is yet to explore, to experience, to play with; the joyous up, the fertile learning ground of down. Don't be in a hurry to awaken. That assumes an end to reach, a line to cross. I have not found one, and I can't come close to imagining how there could ever be one.

Life is showing you the freedom that comes from playing where you are, as you are, without heedless reliance on the stream of chatter running interference.

Any desire to get somewhere or be something is resistance to now, is the separated self, is the illusion of power-knowing-choice.

Some are in over their heads, having jumped into duality feet first; they are treading water so fast that it may take most of their life, and perhaps one or two more to drown, to let the waters of *What Is* have them.

My experience taught the cost and the folly of the default way of living. I know what it's like to tread water, how it feels to barely keep my nose up and the water out of my lungs, to know that inevitably I will tire and sink to the bottom. That's anxiety and exhaustion masquerading as life.

I didn't know then what I know now—that drowning, letting go into the flow, isn't as bad as it seems.

It is quite fun to wait and see, to let the waves run their course, to be effortlessly moved closer to shore or deeper into the depths, wherever life itself takes me.

CHAPTER 11

Time and Space—There Goes the World!

Time is an interesting and useful concept. We use it to navigate our experience but believing it is real can wreak havoc. As soon as you accept that time is real you have sealed your death warrant, not necessarily right now, but sometime in the future, down the linear track from now, from the assumptive moment where you currently find yourself.

Birth and death are concepts based on the appearance and disappearance of a body. It is easy to see how that adds to the mistaken identity of time and space. A baby is born. He or she lives a life with as much time they are given—and then dies. To all the senses, this concretizes the passage of time and the transit of an object that used to take up space. Death occurs, the space becomes empty, and time appears to move on without the loved one, measured now in terms of absence rather than presence.

You can see the progression from baby bump to the casket. Progress. Surely, that's solid evidence of time, isn't it? You base your life around a clock, a calendar, around the appearance of a sun in the sky (space) arriving and departing (time). One day ends as another begins and—just like that—you are a day older. Days to years to lifetimes, smooth skin to wrinkles, birth to death—and you have the semblance of time passing.

Progress: a concept?

Is time actually passing?
    Is there such a thing as time?
    There is no future other than a mental construct called imagination. There is no past other than as a mental construct called memory. You can't go back and kiss the boy in 7th grade again. You can't go forward and see what's around the corner. Time is essential to the material worldview. Without it, there is no world. even though time doesn't seem to have an independent existence. Even in the material world that is based on what we can see and touch, there still is no past we can put our hands on, no future we can embrace.
    As if that weren't enough, there isn't even a present moment, a moment in time you call *now*. By the time a perception or sensation registers it is already a relic of what you call the past. Nothing, not one thing, can be pinned down. There is no one moment in time—past, present, or future—no destination you can visit. You cannot prove time's existence in any tense. Time, and its various specious stages, is simply a useful tool to traverse life with all its minefields and playgrounds that appear in and as elementary, inexplicable experiencing.

Life: a speculation?

Objects seem to appear and disappear. When your beloved slips behind the wheel of the car and drives down the street and out of view, are they still real when you cannot see them?

Were they ever? An hour or two later, they pop back into your line of sight and into your experience again. Can you prove they still existed when they were beyond the reach of perception and the dynamics of sensation? Can you prove that they were ever real, even when they stood before you, other than as a perception, a sensation, a thought? They existed in your imagination and memory. Lots of things exist in imagination and memory but that doesn't make them discretely real.

When you close your eyes, the waking world disappears from sight. You fall asleep and slip into dreamland where new worlds appear. As you drop into dreamless deep sleep, everything disappears—time, the new dream worlds, and the world you call material reality. You can live an entire lifetime in a dream. Time has no meaning in dreamland. When you awaken and look at the clock, five or six hours have passed, or just a few minutes.

If time is real, how is the distortion or cessation of time possible? Dreams, according to the materialist story, have different parameters, but look beyond the easy out. Be daring. What you call time is the experiencing of a seeming progression, experiences mentally linked together and believed to delineate duration. Building words around it, building worlds around it, you call it time, but is it real?

Do dreams have their own condensed or expanded progression of time?

How could you know you slept deeply, that hours passed, without conscious awareness that you did? Where was time while you slept?

Time: a mental construct?

Dreamland offers us a peephole into the fabric of time. It is a grand pointer, a funhouse of mirrors, the feel of intricate, intimate, solid reality posing as the passage of days, hours, months, lifetimes, and egging you on to look closer. The clock's tick within the dream feels real, looks real, seems real—and yet, it is not—but then again, what is real?

The only thing you can ever be somewhat certain of is that experiencing of what seems to be time occurs. Experiencing never disappears, only the activity of seeming progression can vanish, for it is not spacebound, or timebound, or made of material objects, but the nonstop fluctuation of appearances.

Awareness—experiencing this *you are*—is always present. It is *Presence* itself, and is the only reality you can verify. What it actually *is*, now that's an entirely different bag of tricks.

The passage of time in the world of the separate self seems pretty darn real as well. It feels palpably, sensually, achingly real while it is believed. Time appears to pass, but it is relative, just like it is in the material world, only with fewer layers of inflexibility. Time in either world can seem to go slow, or move faster than the speed of sound. You know this. You experience this. You just don't grasp how *thrilling* it is.

Do you want to be thrilled? Then stay tuned!

When you are eagerly anticipating something 'good', time drags interminably as you wait for the day to end. It feels like time is stuck, the second hand on the clock jittering in place … and then you're enjoying yourself, in the flow of excitement and joy, and you wonder where the time went.

Remember when you were a kid? Life seemed

stuck-in-the-mud slow while you were growing up. It felt like you had forever ahead of you, all the time in the world to live and explore, to figure life out. Painful experiences burned as if branded on your forehead, impervious to removal. Once you began experiencing life away from your childhood home, and had children—or pets—of your own, the clock seemed to tick faster, faster still. When you reached fifty, it seemed like you'd fall asleep and be sixty by the time you woke up.

How could anything so relative be real?

There is a simple answer—it's not.

Time was never mere tick marks on the measuring sticks we call clocks and calendars. There was never, is never, will never be anything but experiencing.

Past, present and future disintegrate, taking *then* and *when* with them.

Then never existed other than as an echo. *When* was nothing more than a tease. It was all a magic trick, your vivid imagination assigning reality to a phantom. When we see the relativity of time, when we question the fundamentals of its reality, time just falls apart.

The spacetime cookie crumbles

Without time, space crumbles. They are two expressions of the same creative aliveness, and like everything that can be known, while each appears to be singularly distinct, they are not two. Distance without time or space is non-existent—no *here* and *there*, no progress to be made.

When time and space fall apart, there goes the world ... and you. Perceptions arise. Sensations make their presence known. Thoughts inspire or wreak havoc. Feelings and emotions tug at your heart. Life goes on, experienced more intensely, with a depth that escaped you before.

Seeing time as real extends a high level of viability to a conceptual tool that is of use in negotiating life's twisting, turning illusory labyrinth. It switches what's abstract into the concrete realm. Unnecessary and problematic at best.

Life can be lived quite well, and with gusto, without adding the gloss of reality to a conceptual maze.

CHAPTER 12

The Wow of Now

Time is against the ropes here and the idea of *now* begs for closer inspection. Remaining 'present', 'being in the now', cannot be what they are made out to be—a stitch of time with mystical properties, a moment of *Presence* that opens the doors to truth, that sets everything aright. Time itself is more than a little suspect, so what is *now*?

Now: not a snippet of time

Now is a pointer, a pointer that like all pointers, points to a bigger reality. All life points in one non-directional direction— home to the mystery we are. Every experience sings the praise of *Infinite Aliveness* and that includes the hugely misunderstood concept of the present moment, of *now*.

Now is not a tiny fraction of time in constant movement— catch me if you can.

> *Now* is not something that you can experience if you are exceptionally still. *Now* does not consist of being faithful to what is arising in the immediate moment—not even if you release all ideas of past and future while you engage.

There is no practice you can fine tune until you find yourself at last in the promised land of *now*, for as a practice it is doomed to fail. *Now* as a moment in time cannot be found.

How could you not be present?

Once upon a time I used to talk about the present moment, about *now* as if it were something special, the answer, a grail of sorts. Whenever I would speak about 'remaining present' something always felt off. How could we not be present? Lordy, is that even possible? *Presence* is all there is. I could feel that. I knew that. It just hadn't made it into the world of words yet. That's why it felt wrong. I was in a state of limbo, where what I knew had not broken through the conditioning I had imbibed. I was still holding onto the idea of the present moment as the goal, something to achieve, a prize to lean into. It was still a coveted, very specific, place in time where everything would be okay once I settled in and put down roots. If I could just settle in and put down roots everything would be okay.

Of course, that wasn't possible, so instead of being a healing fix, each time I reminded myself I wasn't present it pumped a fresh supply of need into my veins.

Even if I took time out of the equation—time, an essential variable in the world of separation—I was left with so many questions: *Is there an unlimited supply of nows? How can I remain present if the moment is always moving? And, why does any effort I make to be present feel so damned impossible?*

It didn't make any sense. I knew it was pointing to something important, but I didn't know how to explain it, to put it into words. I hadn't yet seen that *now* is the nothing that is everything. It is awareness itself, intimate, ordinary experiencing.

The prison door swung wide

One Sunday I was leading meditation at OSCI, a men's medium-security prison, and the hype that I'd been trying to defend for so long, the propaganda propping up the present moment came crashing down. I was sharing a quote from *Be Here Now*, by Ram Dass. Suddenly it was clear that each word pointed to the same thing, be … here … now. Each word pointed to experiencing, that for which there is no other, that which is no thing—quite simply described as *now*.

When I stop and notice that I am aware, that there is no separation between me and being aware, no place where I stop and the other begins, where am I?

All that is present is *Presence* itself: nowness, hereness, beingness.

There is no space between now and here, between beingness and experience. There is no space and there is no time. Without the beliefs that I use to decipher my perceptions and sensations, there is naught but essential experiencing.

Now has been misidentified as a fragment of time.

We look outward at the ever-changing scenery, the amazements of life, the content of experience, instead of relaxing our position and stepping into the mystery that is aware of the content and experiencing the display.

Finding your way out of the optical illusion

Seeing what *now* is, is just like that moment when an optical illusion flips, revealing something entirely different and unexpected. It instantly shifts our worldview with a tiny little flutter and a breath-taking surprise, and just like the optical illusion, once you've seen it, you've seen it. You can look away, but it's always right here. Not seeing it is no longer possible.

The display changes, it moves, it appears to be three-dimensional; it's like a movie that is light shining on a two-dimensional screen—pixels of imagination appearing as a world. What is the presence, the nowness, that experiences the movie? *You*, the experiencing. What is the movie? It too is nothing but experiencing.

The killer question

The killer question, the showstopper that follows on from that: is the separate self the experiencer, or part of the field of experience?

My 93-year-old mother looked at me shortly before she passed from this realm, and said: *Why don't I feel 93?* Then she shyly added: *I've never felt my age. Am I crazy?*

She knew. *Now* is not a moment in time.

This *we are* does not age. It is always *now*. There is nothing but *now*, and you are that.

No matter how many acts of this play you experience, *this that experiences* isn't changed at all. Whether my mother knew consciously that she is ageless isn't important. She knew that life was something altogether alien to her old thinking.

How old are you when you don't look in the mirror?

Experiencing has no age, for it is timeless, spaceless. What perceives your story, what experiences your life, is not the separate self, the one who appears to age. The story of aging is an appearance in the play of life and the separate selves, you and me, are characters in the play.

The eyes are a window to the soul, the body is a temple.

They are portals through which *Infinite Aliveness* experiences the illusion of time and space, its joys and delights, the pains and sorrows of being finite, of being human.

CHAPTER 13

Silence and Stillness

How often have you tried to quiet your mind, to still the unending chatter and find inner peace—the silence almost every teacher points to—and how many times have you failed? This is the stark reality for many who try to meditate. Countless beginners just give up, believing that they are different, that they weren't cut from the same pattern as those who can quiet their minds.

They walk away frustrated, thinking that now in addition to the troublesome reasons that brought them to meditation, something else, something spiritually limiting, is wrong with them too. Having been told that silence is the key, that it opens the doors to a higher understanding of life, they feel that their mind is just too busy to find peace, the ceaseless chatter within too strong. The peace and happiness they sought will forever elude them, the possibility of seeing past mind's story gone, evaporated, out of reach. Believing the mind, its stories of limitations and lack, they simply lose heart before they have hardly begun.

What a sad and painful slap in the face!

It happens more often than you'd think. It happened to me when I was first drawn to meditation. It happened because I confused silence with no sound, with the absence of voices in my head, the end of the chattering mind. It happened because I believed the parade of thoughts was my mind, that I had a mind that needed to be controlled, that could be tamed.

What exactly is mind?

Mind isn't some unruly child that you need to discipline. What you call 'mind' is a compilation of thoughts, and thoughts chitter chatter. That's what they do—until they don't, which might never be the case. Minds, or what passes for minds, are creative energy in motion taking the form of thought, thoughts strung together and passing for a definite thing or object which we, with our material world indoctrination, label 'mind.' *Actuality* is quite different from what we think, including the thoughts that assume an identity, and the beliefs on which the identity hangs.

> Mind is not an enemy, not a target to be silenced.

Mind is a concept, an appearance in experiencing, just like the separate self. Mind is conceived through a patchwork of experience. Thoughts are mentally stitched into patterns and craft a mind and a thinker: a mind that is not mind at all but experiencing, a thinker who is but a ghost in the works.

What would happen if you stopped to see what's really going on?

Who does the thinking?

Do you think or do thoughts simply appear? A thought arises

and you think you are thinking it—another thought—and assign it a level of importance—another thought. All of it, the first thought of the series, the identification with the thought, and the assignation of value are all appearances arising in and as experiencing.

It's not wrong getting caught in the games of mind. It is part of the unfolding, the couldn't-be-otherwise field of experiencing, the eternally under-construction blueprint remodeler.

The game of mind experience isn't bad; it is simply limited, confused, and often disconcerting.

Seeing it as the ultimate reality, the end game, is painful—unlike the peace that is your ultimate birthright.

I grew up in a small town in Southern Oregon. When my dad was a kid his family moved every year, sometimes more often. He didn't want that for his children, so we stayed put. In many ways it was a gift, one I couldn't see until I graduated and moved away. In high school, getting out of Small Town USA sat at the top of my priority list. Just for something to do, I'd sit on a raised perch in the trees that overlooked the freeway. I would silently watch the cars and trucks winding down the Interstate Highway, wondering where they were going and wishing I was going with them.

Are your thoughts entertaining, disconcerting—or both?

Watching your thoughts is like that. It is how I finally broke through a meditation block, after I conceded that there wasn't a right way, leastwise not one I could master, that worked. For me, meditation was pretty basic. It was sitting as still as I could and being available to life as it is.

When I first started I was the watcher and that went on for some years.

Then one day something shifted, and *I was the silence watching, the stillness embodied,* the non-moving surrendered presence: not going anywhere, not needing anything.

The years in between seemed like a gradual progression, a slow striptease that peeled away my closely held beliefs, the fallacies based in thought and embodied, held dear and used to ensure that the pain and suffering hung around. Of course, I didn't know that then. I just lived it.

It wasn't actually a straight line, a steady progression. The original pile of beliefs didn't always shrink, sometimes it even grew unnoticed. The sense of progression was a boon to that seeker, delaying her demise. The idea that I was progressing, that I was improving, making headway in the battle for enlightenment, pinned medals on my chest and added gold plating to my armor.

Pitfalls on the path

Spiritual arrogance seems to be a pitfall that few of us avoid completely. It's hard not to feel special, as if meditation is a superpower, when it makes you feel so amazing. Luckily, that class of arrogance also feels fraudulent.

The shift from being the watcher, what some call the witness, to simple silence wasn't something I did. If I had actually been in charge, I would have made darn sure I ended up being special. That's what the identity wants. It doesn't want the truth. Fortunately, the pains of life, the sense of fraud, the craving for authenticity, were prompts that could not be denied, the come-hither call petitioning inquiry into what actually is.

If it is possible to control thought, why can't you?

Do we ever initiate anything? When I began the experiment, I thought the thoughts were mine, that they belonged to me, and then I realized that they were not my slaves. They had no owner. Thoughts simply appeared and disappeared like the cars on the freeways of my youth. Untouched, they would pass me by and keep on moving. Some were fascinating, but they were only in my line of sight for a short time, and quickly replaced by the next. Some made me laugh out loud. Sometimes I got hooked and hopped into the back seat of the sedan headed south, until I realized what I had done and reclaimed my seat in the trees.

Eventually I quit hitchhiking, or at least I didn't stick my thumb out quite as often. The silence watching held greater fascination than the objects passing through. The meditator sitting and trying to meditate, gives way to a witness, a stepped-back watcher watching the meditator and the thoughts. That too eventually morphs, opening into greater silence, into awareness aware of life … Then, in its own perfect timing, it gives way to simple, basic experiencing—no me, no gig, just life life-ing, love loving, experience experiencing.

Experiencing: the direct route

You can walk the long and curvy road from sitter to watcher, watcher to awareness of life, awareness of life to experiencing, or you can skip the prelims and hop straight to experiencing.

Had I known the simple path was possible, I might have taken it instead of the circuitous track I traveled.

It obviously wasn't the path for me, or I would have seen it, would have taken it. Trust needed to build. Willingness to disbelieve my eyes, to let go of what I knew, had to come to a boil and bubble over. Wherever you are, life meets you there. Whatever path you travel into the stillness cannot help but be perfect.

The silence, the stillness that is being pointed to, whether known or not, is the end of the separation of watcher and the watched, of witness and what is witnessed, of awareness and life. Stillness is not the end of chatter, but the end of separation.

Once seen, once this is recognized to be experiencing without an experiencer, the chatter may continue. The soundtrack of experiencing may be far from soundless.

If we expect the chatter to vanish we would be placing a condition on *What Is*; that's a recipe for disappointment, and an invitation that beckons a separate self to stay in business.

Silence vs quiet

The silence you seek is not the quiet. Staying with *What Is*, as it is, the focus shifts from the contents to nowness, to hereness, to experiencing itself. It feels like several steps back from the separate way of being, from outward seeking, and grasping at whatever comes your way.

Whatever appears in awareness, appears. The contents don't matter or at least not in the same way. Freed of the need for life to be a certain way, you can meet the moment with innocent eyes and an open heart. The car is traveling south on the Interstate Highway, and you are not in the driver's seat, not in the back seat, not in the trunk. You are not even in the car.

Your experience is dynamite!

Experiencing—and the recognition it imparts—set off an implosion in your carefully constructed house of cards. It seems so ordinary, an everyday given, and yet once the recognition shifts, or once it starts to shift, it doesn't end until the entire house crashes down.

Meditator and meditation are seen and viscerally felt to be not two, and the idea of a watcher, ludicrous.

The watcher—along with the entire world and all its multitudinous pieces—is known to be shadows of illusion, dreamed characters giving Academy Award winning performances. Bravo! It is a wondrous delusion, and all of it is you.

You are the switch that flips

Meditation is one of countless vehicles that life provides to demonstrate what it really is, what you really are. Sufficiently emptied, meditation drops you into silence, just as extreme sports can drop you into the flow when the rush of everything but the moment falls away. Life is always showing you, opening the way for seeing. Life and all its experiences, the good and the bad, the delightful and the heartbreaking, the playful and the ones that feel like damnably hard work, are nothing but the showing.

Silence is what you are, not something you achieve. Your movement away from life exactly as it is, turns up the volume.

ACTUALITY

Resistance is the noise, for it is the one who seeks. Settling into life as it is, turns the volume down, and then gradually, or instantly in scattered cases, flips the switch to off. When it doesn't matter what content is playing, when you don't mind what happens next, what remains is what always was, silence, hiding in plain sight, no longer amplified by ideas of escape.

Slipping into the stillness, if only occasionally, makes you more available to the question: *What is experiencing?*

If you can be *here*, be *now*, simply *be*, you can catch a glimpse of the true mystery.

CHAPTER 14

Feeling

You think you are in touch with your life, that you are feeling what is here for you to feel. When a radical friend—and only a radical friend would ask such a question—asks you to reach down deep and feel your experience you'd swear that's what you are doing.

Nothing could be further from the truth!

What you feel is not what's actually here, the primacy, the stunning beauty inherent to experiencing, its rich ethereal absolute insubstantiality. You don't feel how elusive experience is, that it can't be pinned down, that it isn't something you can name, let alone know. If you did, you would see the miraculous in every breath.

Thoughts, in the guise of beliefs, preconceptions, misconceptions and misinterpretations, color and shade your experience inside the lines of what you believe possible. You don't believe what you see; you see and feel what you believe. You cannot feel and sense, let alone intimately *grok* what is outside your current sets of beliefs and preconceptions. Instead of meeting experiencing directly, you look to the contents of experience and cannot, will not, meet that without wrapping it in a weighted blanket to soften the sharp edges.

Where do you stash your monsters?

You label your heartache, the wounds of this lifetime, the stuffing—the festering hurts you have stuffed down deep inside, the monsters pounding on the closet door trying to get out. In that labeling you create new monsters outside of you, ones that point fingers away from you, away from your innermost experience, and miss the shimmer that permeates this grand illusion, the mystery of experiencing.

Rather than feeling the nuanced depths—*Infinite Aliveness*—you leap over it to the contents of your blanketed experience, and plow right past the truth of it to something less threatening. What you feel in the place of the miracle that you truly are is layers down; it is not even the content of your experience but your resistance to it.

You feel through layers of fantasy, stories you have created to blunt the truth of your aching heart. You feel through the armor, the chain mail of separation. You feel the lie all dressed up and out on the town, a sorry pantomime of life. Often, that is all you are capable of feeling. Some of us are so disconnected by our wounds all we can feel is the numbness that has set in.

Does separation blunt the pain? (The answer is *No!*)

You have learned to live in a shell of hardened resistance that you unwittingly designed to keep yourself safe, that you think keeps you from coming face to face with the wounds to your psyche that you have instinctively tried to suture with baling wire.

When you feel, when feeling escapes from where you have

exiled it, you feel the dust of what was, the remnants of the storms that have passed, your regrets and your hopes, but rarely, if ever, do you allow yourself to feel what you have tucked into the inner sanctum, let alone the wonder of life.

That is the reason you ache. It is what's behind the yearning for something more. The unwillingness, the inability to face each moment unprotected, to meet what you truly are, lies at the heart of your heartache.

You crave authenticity, and fear to be foolish, to let down your guard, to live life as it comes with full-on honesty. You want to be real. You are so very tired of the game of pretend, of pretending you are okay, that you aren't scared, that life doesn't hurt, and it's all going to work out ... somehow. Ironically, for the pretender that is, you cannot not feel, cannot not experience.

You are feeling. You are experiencing. You feel *What Is*, or you feel your resistance to it. Either way—you feel.

Fear not! Breathe life in and *feel!*

Contrary to many spiritual teachings, you are only a breath away from freedom, peace, and happiness, whatever your state of disconnection. Granted, it is a big breath, one that requires you to open into what you are feeling when what you are feeling is the pain of your wounds and the fear that tries to swamp your resolve, or worse, your stories of redirection.

You do not need to have completed years of spiritual work and successfully cleared out the layers of defiance first. You simply need to see the futility of walking down the same dead-end road.

ACTUALITY

When the pain is big enough, the risk feels less intimidating. Instead of remaining tight in the bud, you open and dip beneath the surface, feeling more of what is here to feel, placing a toe in the lotus pond.

You may not be ready to step all the way in, especially when what is present is frustration and anger, doubt and self-loathing. Those feelings are not erroneous even though they are not the truth of you. They are your experience, not something to overcome. They are the exceptional experiences that brought you to the dawning of possibility. Like all experiences, they are a gateway, an invitation to test the water, to decompress even a tiny bit and see what life is.

Lying in bed, feeling the shocks ripple through my system, mostly in a state of non-resistance, a very basic thought came to mind, "What if this was all you had ever known, what if life had never been any other way than it is right now, shocks and all?"

That smidge of awareness, a glimmer of light in the darkness, opened into the recognition of the clear slate that lies under the plane of thought. It dropped me into innocent wonder, into a precious willingness to see what's here before my mind takes over. I could clearly see the stories I had written, and it was astonishing to me how blatantly obvious they were. It was like someone turned a light on and I was no longer groping my way through the darkness.

The stories protected me from experiencing what's here, my life as it is, shocks included. They put layers of padding over what's present, smothering pure experiencing. I didn't feel my life. I felt my stories about my life. Actuality, the *Infinite Aliveness*, is fully available before our interpretations and impressions pile on, before they consciously or unconsciously deaden our experience. Suppression seems to be an unavoidable part of life, unavoidable but not mandatory.

Instead of writing and rewriting my personal stories about the shocks, I felt them as they were. The need to make them wrong, to understand them, to validate or repudiate, to blame and shame, bypass or integrate, to do any of the practices and techniques I had learned through the years was replaced by a grounded willingness to experience life exactly as it is.

This was not a mental practice. It was wholly physical.

I followed the shocks as they created new pathways through this body. I exploded with the energy as each shock reached its crescendo, as it met the end of its surge. There was nothing but the energy, the feeling, sensations of varying intensity: the quick blast, the soft ripple, the out of nowhere pulse. Without the story it was all just energy moving. Not attaching meaning, the stuff of interpreted significance, the stories evaporated, no longer necessary.

The willingness to meet life in its fullness needs no stories for they merely get in the way.

It's not always easy or possible to meet our experience, especially when it's filled with pain. We are inherently programmed to push back against it. It's primal, the urge to survive ... and it's societal, trained into us from the time we pushed out of the womb. Seeing it, even after the fact of the push-back, we have the opportunity to stop, to meet it, to feel the sensations at the core. Our unique experience, the same one we curse, deny, and deride, is the magic potion, the mother of all remedies. It is *Infinite Aliveness*. It is the magic carpet ride we seek. It's just not the trip most of us desire.

Meeting what's here is more difficult from the contracted state. Contraction is resistance, the homeland of the separate self. In the body it often looks like knots of stress, inflamed bumps under the skin, or overall physical tightness, like a boa constrictor dropped down from the trees to give you a squeeze. It is both physical and mental, a way of interacting with the world that is rigid and inflexible. Still ensconced within the need to resist, you have yet to build up the trust muscle, to see the power of allowing your experience to be. Even without that preparation, regardless of where you find yourself, stressed and contracted or not, it is still possible to stop and engage life as it is.

Are you ready to see your fear?

Once you realize that your resistance and your actions stem from fear, then opening to another possibility, even one you denigrated a moment ago, is a natural progression. The leading edge of recognition has worn a hole in the wall of self-protection. Your previous reference points for how to do life begin to break up and fall away, and what's left, the only move remaining, is to meet life as it is.

It starts small even though it feels big. Each new crack, each breakthrough feels like a homerun, like you finally dove across home plate. Hang on; stay with it. Recognition expands like popcorn popping in a pan—and sometimes just as fast!

You realize that what you seek is not a target that can be acquired, but symphonic movement beyond any meaning conveyed in words.

The rest of the stuffing begins to fall out once the soft

targets, the more conscious stories you invented, crumble. All the old feelings you've wedged within make their way into conscious experience. You detained them unknowingly because you weren't capable of meeting them as they arose. You hadn't had the requisite life experiences to prepare you.

Your inability to meet your feelings in the moment compressed the aliveness and stuffed it away until you were ready. You were not able to feel them; now you can. Being ready doesn't mean you won't be intimidated by what's happening, or that it will be fun and easy. It just means that you are more skilled at meeting whatever arises.

Whatever arises ... meet that

Little by little you open up, feeling child-like anger one second and happiness the next, holding onto nothing beyond the inmost breath, the intimate feel of experience, and letting it pour through you. Things happen and in that moment are felt, are directly experienced.

It is astounding. What you feared proves not to be what you thought at all. What is here right now, freed of the unwillingness to feel, is *Infinite Aliveness* masquerading as loss and ache, imprisonment and grief, as every storyline of humanity's chains and joys.

Now you engage with your experience and recognize the very aliveness you are. You tend to what's in front of you, to what's within you. You open to feeling what is here, not for some higher purpose, but because it is what is here, and what is here is the only reality you can even slightly lend credence to.

This experience as it is, is your grail and there is nothing you can point to, nothing that has any reality but this. All else is supposition, a shadow in the illusionist's game. You've been there. Remember? You took the game of shadows off your list.

What's real?

Experience is reality and feeling into it, experiencing what it is, reveals the miracle of life that was never hidden, that was always staring you in the face: experience—life—is the mystical madness, the indefinable enigma. Beyond that, beyond the immediacy of experiencing, not one word can be said with any accuracy.

To put experiencing into words is impossible, and despite the impossibility, attempts appear. They too, are the sweet voice of experiencing, prolific yet bound-to-flounder pointers destined to make the rounds and come full circle back to themselves.

This *That Is* is its multiplicity of self-expression, its infinite dance of life.

Experiencing alone *is*, and the nature of what it is reveals itself as we openly encounter our experience, feeling whatever occurs. Many prefer to use words such as 'isness', 'consciousness' or 'awareness', rather than experiencing, but those terms seem to discount the messy human side of the equation, and leave the concept of separation a bit more intact. Experiencing feels more all-inclusive. It points to the nerve center of life that feels all of its angels and demons, that is grounded in the invisible and the visible.

Feeling the darkness reveals what the darkness is

The felt sense of separation, while a mass of very convincing sensations, was never a viable separate being. It is a tin god, a concept comprised of circular logic wrapped in sensations of resistance. A product of make-believe, a stand-in to tamp down the terror of absolute uncertainty, the separate self falls apart like dandelion seeds spread by the winds of experience when directly felt. Nothing but a thought in a stream of thoughts, that which never was disintegrates.

Feeling, even when it is resistance you feel, when genuinely, emptily, touched sensed explored, takes you into the heart of experience, into that which alone is. It doesn't matter if you still owe fealty to the separate self, or if you have already seen through it, even if only mentally. Uncensored, raw feeling takes you directly to experiencing and flips the optical illusion to reveal the garden's open gate.

Feeling what's here right now, regardless of what that is, is an act of utmost courage. You either turn and face your experience or continue to turn away from it. Once you realize that turning away still hurts, that your heart hasn't stopped aching, that you are slowly dying despite your best efforts, the beliefs holding the false identity in place start to dissipate.

You feel what's actually here, or you feel what you have been conditioned to see as real—the secondhand reality; or you feel your misdirected redirects—the stories you make up about secondhand reality. All ways, always, you feel. There is no escape.

CHAPTER 15

The Persistent Myth of Choice

You'd probably rather I skip this chapter. It's a powerful belief, usually one of the last ingrained fallacies to fall. So I'll say it plain and quick. There are no mistakes ... and yes, you are not mistaken, *no mistakes* points directly to *no choice*.

There is the appearance of free will, but it is only an appearance, an important feature of the dream of separation.

Everything is an appearance, is experiencing, so why would choice be real when nothing else is.

What fun would it be if you knew this was a dream, that the game is rigged? Honestly ... a whole lot of fun. Realizing that life is a holographic theme park ride changes the entire experience.

Not choosing—still a choice

Once you are aware of this feature you continue to act as if you have choice, for it truly seems you do, and more importantly, you couldn't choose not to. That would be a choice, now wouldn't it?

You couldn't choose to quit making decisions if you wanted to. Even from the standpoint of a material world, deciding not to act is still a decision.

To those standing on the outside looking in, it looks like nothing has changed. Choice points crop up, you decide which way to move, and head in the 'chosen' direction. The big change is internal. You know that it's all an illusion, a very real illusion, choice included. It has illusory reality. It feels real and seems to make a difference, to make a real impact. A plus B continues to add up to C ... or D, depending on your version of math.

The choices you make are based on your model of the world. You will not intentionally choose to hurt someone if your model of the world is compassionate, while if your model is winning at all costs you won't consider another's feelings or needs. The conditioning chooses.

For choice to exist you would have to control the million little things, many of which are sub- or unconsciously affecting the choice; you don't control them, how could you!

Depending on your world model, you might have compassion for the painful choices I make, or you might think my life is a waste of breath. In a world where there are no mistakes, how could my apparent choices be wrong? Even if I spent my entire life surveying the realms of hell, which it feels like at times, nothing could be amiss.

Life is *doing life* ... whether it's a prison sentence or not is up for grabs

What you experience, you experience. It couldn't be otherwise. The inner conditioning, the outer circumstances, the entirety of life chooses. Experiencing itself, and its specific contents, are the all-knowing guru. Could you say that anyone's experience is better than another's? One might be more comfortable, more comforting, but even that is colored with conditioning. What you might see as fortuitous, I might see as deranged. Regardless of content, all experiences are sacred experiencing.

It seems to be easier to notice what this is when the ocean waves are not as rough and capricious, but even that seemingness is blind. Who truly knows what will trigger the recognition? Noticing is possible as long as experience is present, and it is never absent.

Why? Why? Why?

In my model, the purpose of incarnation is to recognize what life is. Why? Because it opens, enhances, upgrades the experience of being in a body in ways that are unfathomable until the truth of what we are is physically grounded, physically not simply as a mental exercise. The body is necessary. In an earthly incarnation, the physical is more than important, it is critical. It is the instrument of sensation and feeling, the perceiver and receiver of light.

The body is your compass, telling you when you are aligned with truth and when you are off course.

Additionally, and just as importantly, all of life appears to lean in the direction of revelation. It is constantly presenting experiences that shake up the status quo, that break up the reliance on separation. It feels like life wants to be found out, to be recognized for what it is.

The infinitely evolving blueprint chooses

If being enamored of the contents of experience, caught up in the highs or lows, distracts from the noticing, then that's what it does. In that moment, recognition of *What Is* isn't in the cards for that particular human expression. Yes, the experience could be even more magnificent if *Actuality* was deeply recognized, but it wasn't. It couldn't be given the resident blueprint. The experience of what this is remains elusive, and yet the not seeing is still illusive but in a slightly more hellish way.

No one is wrong or right. No one gets the credit or the blame, for no one chooses. This is the outer expression of perpetual synchronous adaptation. The plan's lines, both visible and hidden, move and re-form with each new experience, each new breath. You cannot change the inner and get a better outer, because you don't choose what changes. Your experiences change the blueprint. All experiences change the blueprint, experiences which no one chooses ... and everyone appears to choose. Each experience adds to and updates the data field which alters the buildout in the projected world.

Would you really choose the bad stuff? Honestly?

Experiences choose you. Would you choose cancer even if you knew that while the illness ravaged your body it would open you in ways that you could not imagine, that it would secrete appreciation for life unlike anything else? Would you make the decision to experience blindness, bankruptcy, or homelessness, even if you knew they would radically intensify the trajectory of spirit? Most of us would not, although there are a few crazies amongst us.

You love life. You want to live longer. You want comfort and ease. Choosing hardship for most would be a hard no ... and yet, cancer lives in this world of separation, along with freezing to death in make-shift tents, napalm, chemical warfare and nuclear bombs, starvation and child molestation. If you can choose, you choose everything. If you don't, you can choose nothing. There is no on-again, off-again switch, no compromise available to add a little deadener to the uncertainty, except in your imagination.

You do not know what's coming next. Your plan—any plans—may fall apart. You adapt or you don't, and new plans take shape.

You get where you are going, and the whole thing falls apart or goes in a new and surprising direction. You don't control life, and if you are the tiniest bit open you already know this. You just don't want it to be true.

Is anyone really in charge?

Whether you will be positively, negatively, or neutrally impacted by these words already resides within the blueprint. Whether I will write these words, or go for a walk in the woods with my pup, is also in the blueprint. In a very real way, this book and your reaction to it are fully formed inside of you, inside the pool of energy that you are before the words are loosed into the field of experiencing.

Some of you will resonate with these words. Some may be

repelled by the very idea of them. We are all a divine puzzle made of uniqueness and singularity. The field is replete with the multiplicity of possibilities, and in its wholeness it is singular.

Experiences form within the field and, not unlike a hurricane, the energetic intelligence signature of the blueprint shifts, gathering sufficient momentum to spin into manifestation as a new entangled human data field. The human, and the field of intelligence, are not separate. Manifestation does not point to disconnection. They are symbiotic, conjointly informing and being informed, an unending exchange of intelligence. In concert, assigning the nature of the roles to be played, they are constantly shifting variables awash in a sea of change.

What manifests is not punishment for bad works, nor it is a reward for good behavior. Experiences are what they appear to be in the apparently physical world, and yet, they are not that at all ... both simultaneously. What you see as a material world is a multitude of expressions, their sentient and non-sentient receptors, spiraling up, spiraling down, infinity loops of interactive, integrated symbiosis.

There is *not-two*—experience and you, the awareness and that guy appearing to be a waste of a good incarnation. Only experiencing is. The content of experience is a set-up, set up in this moment based upon the infinite model's current state and the eternal state of change.

CHAPTER 16

Incarnation—Reincarnation

With so many fallacies under suspicion, reincarnation's tenets can now be inspected without a filing cabinet of misconceptions getting in the way. Reincarnation focuses on a discrete essence that takes on a new form based on the old form's progress or regression, so you can see the inherent difficulty. Although it is interpreted various ways across different religions, its basic doctrine is that your next life is chosen by the actions of your past lives, a sort of post-mortem punishment or reward.

Without choice, if the unique expressions of the singularity are recycled, the stinger of personal responsibility is removed. Progress is also thrown out, since its possibility, other than as an appearance, falls apart with time and space. The separate being, once seen to be a very real illusion, has no need to reincarnate, no lessons to learn, nothing to overcome. It is but a grand character in the play of life.

Could the appearance of the separate self be reused, like a used car, a vehicle to explore, to experience? Of course ... why not? Anything is possible. The mystery is the mystery. The idea though, of assigning it an inmate's number, of crime and punishment, is more than a little suspect.

Life after death as punishment or reward in the non-reincarnation camps loses its bite too. How could you have done anything differently? You didn't choose to eat the apple. There is the appearance of choice, not actual choice. How could anyone go to hell or get a free pass to heaven in a rigged game?

Life after death, or life after life?

Hell is putting your faith and trust in separation. Heaven and hell aren't somewhere else; they are right here, right now. There is no *there* or *where* to go, no *then* or *when* to go there, no experience other than this *Infinite Aliveness*, this simple experiencing.

Each expression is a one-off, a precious once in any lifetime formation, and yet you aren't just the data points that animate the life you call yours.

What you are is unending metamorphosis, the leaf and the caterpillar, the cocoon and the appearance of time passing, the butterfly and the sky—the entirety if there were such a thing.

All visible expressions—what you call 'you' and 'me', and 'the world'—are reflections mirroring the degree of alignment with *What Is*, the *Isness* of life. The various gradations of alignment: the emptiness of resistance, the innocent simplicity of awareness, or the full-to-overflowing cup of knowing that spins the hamster wheel, all these reflect the expression's experience of life.

You are having an individual experience, but you are not an individual. Just like your precious, sometimes beyond-difficult life, ideas of an afterlife or future lives are based in the world of a separate individual. Such ideas are based in the dream.

Your vehicle of exploration is not reincarnated and reborn, or destined for your particular version of heaven or hell. There is no life after death for an individual. There is only *Infinite Aliveness* taking shape, assuming form.

Splintered truths: life and death as seen through the eyes of separation

The afterlife and reincarnation are misperceptions of a greater reality. The separate self is the craving for life, the desire to go on living, the resistance to death. Deep inside the idea of separation, the birthless, deathless *Actuality* you are knows that death is not real. That's why you can envision something more, can entertain the possibility of something after, and struggle to make it real. You mistake that inner knowing for continuity of the separate self, just like the apparent continuity of thought which you call time.

This *you are* creates and recreates itself in new forms, the movement of light and shadow, the dance of color and shape, eternally, infinitely. You are all-encompassing, non-discriminating absolute potential in motion. You include all possibilities, all forms, all expressions. One expression, one form, is not better than any other form or expression, although it appears that way through the lens of awareness that bets on individuation.

Some expressions are reflections of love; others reflect fear. Take care not to judge, for not one of us sits at the controls. Those whom we respect or revere as masters—Jesus, Buddha, Krishna, Mohammed, Quan Yin and others—were pure reflections, but even they were not the ultimate truth, for they were mirroring the truth of their times. To overlay their words onto our times, is not merely inaccurate, it has potential for harm, for it paints a world stuck in a holding pattern, murdering the ever-changing moment.

Beware of pre-packaged truth

Life—the field of experiencing—is always in motion, a living expression of that which cannot be expressed or communicated.

Dogmatic writings—yesterday's experience set to words—are not filled with aliveness.

Instead, drink of the living word that is within you, that fills you up and spills into the world anew.
    Once one field of experiencing appears to die it breaks up slowly, returning to the oceanic field, the field without beginning or end, the field from which all manifestation flows. How slowly? That question is only of interest to a timebound self. Timelessness doesn't follow time's rules of slow or fast, now and then.
    It is an interesting question though, the kicker, if you will. I speak to my beloved Kenny often. I see him. I feel him. He left this plane—what we call dying—many years ago in Earth time but not even a sparkle in timelessness.

If there is no time, what does that mean for immortality?

Does something of us remain? Are identities eternal? In timelessness this moment still is ... and is not, never having been. When I visited Chaco Canyon and stood by the remains of a once grand *kiva*, built centuries ago by the Pueblo people, I was told by its spirit that I could ask a question, so of course I did. I asked: *What was it like to live here?* The response, immediate and quite powerful: *You've asked the wrong question. You should have asked, what is it like to live here?*

The only reaction to the question of our eternal identities that makes any sense, although nothing truly makes sense, is I don't know. It seems to be as close to accurate as I can get. In fact, it has become my go-to answer for most everything. I guess we'll have to die to find out. As for me, I'm willing to wait and see.

CHAPTER 17

Futility

When disasters strike and your world is turned upside down, the beliefs you rely on desert you. Your previous techniques and tactics fall short, failing to produce as advertised. Everything they pointed to, the way life should be, reveals the plain uncertainty underlying the lies. Even though the sense of futility may not be conscious, it is present.

Disasters empty you and show you how little you really know. They demonstrate the inherent fallacy in what you thought possible, in what you hoped could never happen, or at least not happen to you.

Futility is not a failure of your humanity, not even a failure of your imagination. It is a sacred milestone on the path to discovering what life is, what you are.

Usually, you get a small glimpse of futility before the customary mental meanderings shore themselves up and take over again. Eventually though, you reach the point of flat-out futility. You recognize that nothing you do, nothing you say or think, nothing at all will save you. You realize that you can't delay the inevitable one second. You can't stop the clock. You can't save your loved ones, and the harder you try, the more life taunts you with the unmitigated ineffectiveness of trying to grab that pesky prize.

Are you there yet? Have you reached the point of futility?

This recognition is monumental. It feels hopeless, it may usher in a dark night of the soul, but it is not what it feels like. Hope is but a wish for the future, a fantasy set in time, a storybook ending for a struggling character. It is part of the poison, not the antidote, and there's no need to mourn its demise. The realization of futility is the divine trumpeter, whose fanfare signals the end of hope.

Hope's end is a moment of brilliance, the end of the struggle, a new beginning.

When hope dies, when you reach the point of utter futility, you have come to a fork in the infinitely diverging road, a pass through to a different kind of experience. Is hope bad? Not at all. To one insufficiently prepped to receive the gift of futility, an offering of hope when all seems lost can be a blessing, can stop the slide into lethal hopelessness. Holding out hope though, can also keep you on the treadmill, blinding you to what's really here.

Your experiences up to now illuminate the road marker, lighting the path to be taken. All the happenings of life are part of experiencing, and you don't choose whether to go right, left, or straight ahead. Whether the fork you take detracts from the recognition of what this is or not, is an echo of your experiences, a perfect reflection of the overarching blueprint's current impressions, the out-picturing of the unfolding mystery.

If you do still have hope—don't despair!

Hope, a separator, a feature of separation, hangs around for as long as it does. Experiencing however, must eventually dash it upon the rocks of revelation, for it like everything known is a mirage, a very real mirage, but a mirage nonetheless.

Difficult times, like disasters that try your resilience and push you beyond where you thought you could go, are simply part of the unfoldment of experiencing. They either crack you open, or your avatar (to use online parlance) closes down in a protective stance, reinforcing the identity of a self who can be harmed by the hardship. Opening affords you the opportunity to see more clearly. Closing down takes you further into the separation story.

The separation-based distortion passes through without setting up permanent residence unless you grab onto it. Paradoxically, wanting and avoiding are both ways in which you can grab ahold. If the distortion resonates, then the energy reappears in a mercurial procession of stories, even though it is not archived within. The collections of thoughts, the stories that appear, take center stage until something out of the norm triggers movement to upgrade, degrade or disintegrate that bit of resonant data. Alternatively, it may move you away from the contents—the story—to pure experiencing. Whether you grab or not is not up to you. It's up to life itself.

Do you really know what you're going to do next?

If pandemics, environmental catastrophes, and unscrupulous politics have taught us anything, it's that we don't know each other, or ourselves, nearly as well as we thought. You can never know another. Residing in separation, you can only know your version of another, not what's real to them.

You don't even know yourself. You are clueless about what you are going to do next, especially when your norms are challenged. All that you know, or think you know, is based on what came before. You like to think that you can predict what you'll do next based on your past actions, but you are not a spreadsheet, nor are you any conceivable formula. You are not in control of which new experience will pop up, never mind what you'll do when it does.

That alone should cause you to stop and question reality, to flirt with futility. *Just what is this? What is this thing I call experience anyway, and why won't it behave? If I am the only one who knows my world at all, if I can only slightly know myself, nothing I believed makes sense. How could anything ever be true?*

Humans generally don't stop. We don't question. We keep our seats on life's rollercoaster until the ride gets too scary, until something bad happens, until we reach the top, if not the bottom, of futility and hope drops away.

When life is undeniably out of control you are faced with a hopelessly fabulous opportunity.

Tough times are pregnant with possibility

Futility isn't revealed when you are full of hope. It is found wrapped up in life's tough times, when the world's disasters, and the littler ones, the personal ones that don't feel little at all, take over your life. They reset you, opening you to the cosmic reality that you truly have no control, and if you dared to look closely, that who you think you are is dubious too.

Disasters are one of the many charms beckoning the cobra within, summoning the rising kundalini, the opening that points to another reality.

I couldn't stop Kenny, my husband of twenty years, from dying no matter how hard I tried. Lying next to him in bed, night after night I was tormented by a recurring dream that was intensely frustrating, impossibly futile. I was running down a school corridor trying to catch up to seven *beings* of light who walked ahead of me. Try as I might, I could never reach them.

The corridor morphed from dream to dream. One night it felt like it would squeeze the life out of me. The next it was so vast I couldn't make out the edges. The floor shifted too, from feeling like I was running in quicksand, to the sensation of slipping on tiny balls of glass. I, the dreamed character, knew if I could just catch up, if I could tap those incredible *beings* of light on the shoulder and turn them around, they would teach me what I needed to know. They would give me something I didn't already have, and Kenny would be healed.

Needless to say, I never made it. They were always just out of reach.

Dreams always point

The dream wasn't about being or knowing enough. It wasn't even about being awake enough (my hypothesis at the time). It wasn't about any of the things I considered likely. It was about categorical inability, the utter lack of control, the nature of life on this round blue ball of rock, features of the dream I wasn't yet willing to examine. The dream, like every experience, was a pointer aimed straight at *Actuality*.

That's the beauty of separation, and of clearly seeing

what it is, of seeing the futility in most of what you take to be true. It allows you to know yourself, what you truly are. Your experiences—experiencing itself—juxtapose what you believe, the things you think you know, your faith in separation, with what is actually right here, right now, not hidden at all—your barefaced life.

The divine contrast is never absent. It is always present, for it is *Presence* itself. It is the nature of experience, the surprisingly ordinary holy fractal graphic display, the view of separation from the reality of not-two.

If it's grabbing your attention, then pay attention

Disasters are a powerful expression of *Presence*. They are costumes that clothe the infinite, red-carpet attention grabbers that shake you awake only to overwhelm your senses, to leave you holding an empty bag of futility.

What is futility? It is having nothing left—no convictions to shore up the uncertainty, no preferred way to move forward, no wish to get what you want.

For just a second, or longer if you dare, be simple uncluttered experiencing. From that wide open window into the world it is possible to experience anything without beliefs, opinions, and hopes; without a body that is believed to be separate, conscious and material; without a material world and material others.

It's not as insane as it sounds.

You may get a glimpse, or fall all the way down the bottomless rabbit hole. That's the reality of *Actuality*. You never know where it will take you. Separation, the experience of death and dying, grief and loss, of happiness and joy, aliveness and embodiment in a world that will end, where time doesn't stand still and loved ones depart from you, is present until it brings you to the point of unconditional futility.

You can still live a brilliant life

It is quite possible to experience the entirety of life's panorama with the understanding of what this is, what you are, without the sense of separation. Unexpectedly, it is a richer, deeper, more painful, more joyful experience.

Tears fall more easily. Pain is still felt but differently. Sadness passes by unaccompanied by the stories of loss and lack. Because of that it doesn't seem to stay long. Happiness is, well suffice it to say, unfiltered in any way.

There is nothing but this experiencing having the experience of all the cracks, crevices, boulders, and pebbles of life. Labels and beliefs belong to the thought-stream and are as much an aspect of experiencing as anything else. Nonetheless any attempt at suppression disregards, discounts and disrespects the inherent *thisness*, the stunning mystery at its heart. We humans tend to relate to what we can actually see—a sick lover or a sick self, an ecosystem barely holding on, the extremes of partisanship that delay or arrest positive change—the reality before our eyes, until we are shaken to our cores by the arrival of what we dreaded.

Disaster: grace and peace to you. Futility: permission to come on in.

CHAPTER 18

Preferences: Do They Matter?

The separate self holds many preferences, both subtle and obvious. Such bias is based on an essential inequity, the belief that one version is better than another. These preferences are ways our separated self covertly clings to separation: subtle, crafty ways that fortify the self without appearing to do so. Preferences aren't as solid as beliefs or desires. Right? They're more flexible. They have a bit of bend to them. You don't go to war over your preferences ... or do you?

Preferences, unlike beliefs, are generally out in the open. If you are looking, they are pretty tough to avoid. You don't tend to hide them from yourself because they are 'innocent'. They don't seem as significant as the more insidious stuff of hardened beliefs.

A while back, a friend wrote me a note about time. It was quite interesting, and yet I nearly missed the unique perspective her words suggested. The note was fascinating, using words I probably wouldn't have employed. Rather than connecting with the message, I noticed my preference for other words. Among a few others, she used the word 'space' where I would have used the word 'awareness'—not a big deal—pretty silly in the scheme of things.

Embrace those teaching moments in your life

For that part of me entangled in separation, in the guise of the superiority of my words, that moment was one of life's conscious teaching moments. It was easy to understand the gist of what she was pointing to, but I was blinded by my preference. Instead of entertaining the possibility of something fresh and fun, I spun around in my mythical, far worthier use of words for a moment or two.

In that moment, in simple conversation, did her preferred word really matter? It seemed to, at least in the world where my personal opinion meant something, but this was more. It touched that place of rightness within me, the sensation of failure, of unworthiness. If I let it stand without challenging it, I was somehow less. Preferring one word over another, nitpicking the inconceivable, niggling over phrasing, finding fault with that which cannot be definitively put into words, misses the juicy center the words point to—the meaning being negotiated—but more so, the *Isness* of the experience. It repurposes the experience to one of resistance and inflexibility, and renders the likelihood of meeting the *What Is* of experience, less likely.

The experience of our own preferences, whether met or unmet, is rarely pleasant, the unmet being more obvious than the met. While the satisfied preference might be missed entirely—getting your way tends to cloak the bias—the unmet holds disappointment within it by default. However, any preference encapsulates the hazard of letdown—if not this time, possibly the next.

Do you listen to your body?

The discomfort points directly at the non-aligned, separate act of a confused and misinformed self. The body doesn't lie. It mirrors the truth of who we are. Its comfort or discomfort is the measure of our harmony, or lack of harmony, with life as it is.

You do the same with the people you encounter and you do it automatically. You shut down the miraculous flow by making judgments as to their value and suitability. It's all about *you* not about them: do they they meet *your* preferential standards, do they fit *your* profile? And so you miss out on the complex simplicity, the masterpiece of living and loving that experiencing is. You go right to the illusory form and blow past the formless, the delicious reality permeating your precious life. It's an unavoidable behavior for those who trust in separation.

Seeing all this clearly is a cleansing, a wiping clean of the judgmental slate, a washing out of the filters that divide and separate, if only for a moment.

Preferences are not bad or good in themselves. But, until we have seen through the subterfuge, until we have recognized what is really going on here—even afterwards while the recognition is permeating and rewriting every cell—preferences are the agents of separation, they offer a way to maintain the sense of superiority or inferiority, whichever is our primary conditioning.

Avoidance doesn't work for long

The raw memory, the memory resonating in the history of

being misunderstood, unwanted, and excluded, is founded in the sense of separation. It creates an instinctive neediness that displays as preference, which balances precariously between judgment when the preference is not met and pats on the back when it is. It's tricky, providing seemingly legitimate justification to believe in a separate self, one who succeeds and fails. Using the pull of old emotions and ghostly appearances, it certifies the fallacy, projecting what was onto what is. Preferences come from neediness and that neediness is an instinctive response to our raw memory of being misunderstood, unwanted and excluded.

Neediness and preferences manifest as 'negative' judgement or 'positive' little pats on our back—take your pick, because both the 'negative' and 'positive' legitimize the denial of our true reality.

Seeing the preference in the moment is the noticing, the realization that you are making it up, and if you are making it up, you don't have to do it anymore. Noticing, you are instantly consciously experiencing rather than ruminating about the experience. You are present to *What Is* and what is present at the moment is the preference. The experience of preference is not a lesser experience. Like all experience, when met directly it is an intimate encounter with aliveness itself.

Noticing, you see that you habitually insulate your interactions with a layer of preference. The experience of preference, while still the sacred chalice of experience, tends to contract, to wall you off from life, disengaging you from the raw experience. It feels like a shut-off valve being tightened down until it severs connection. That feeling is a demonstration of separation, showing you what the belief does, how it acts on you, what it is sensorially.

Noticing is magic in motion

Like all of life, noticing is the magnificent teacher. Simply noticing puts a crack in the armor that was created to shield the raw nerve, the memory of hurt, the wound that created a sense of neediness. The crack initiates and ensures that the armor, the thought-created protective covering, will in perfect timing shatter into the billion pieces it never was.

Preferences do matter, mattering right into manifestation. They take form, the form of resistance to *What Is*, of objection to the experience in front of you. They are a head turner, a heart closer, a damper on happiness, war instead of peace. Preferences are also data for the blueprint for they are *Infinite Aliveness* too, and depending on whether they are noticed and directly experienced, not noticed at all, or noticed and ignored, the blueprint shifts accordingly.

CHAPTER 19

A Bad Rap

Duality gets such a bad rap, but honestly, where would you be without its many appearances? Any experience, anything known, anything written or spoken even when it's about non-duality appears as duality. Duality is the precious prize, the magnificent playground, the paradox of paradoxes, the literal gift of a lifetime. Recognizing what it is—and what it isn't—is priceless.

Once duality is seen as a marvelous expression of *Actuality*, rather than the entirety, there is no contradiction within the shift of focus between the apparent two. It seems that is all these human expressions really are—shifts in focus. When the light of beingness is narrowly focused you appear to be a separate self. It is not wholly accurate. It's just how it seems. The focus narrows from the infinite to the finite, taking on the role of a pinhole viewing port in an infinite extravaganza.

When we abide as aliveness, as simple experiencing—even for a moment—the view is no longer limited, no longer fragmented. Nothing is lost; nothing is destroyed. It's more like a movie screen, or a living snapshot—one stunning perception, complete with all the glorious sensations, the moving parts. There's apparent time to progress, to age, to love, to grieve. Space for not only this world, but countless galaxies and dimensions is present. Anything that can be known appears in and as experiencing. The noticeable difference: the absence of a separate experiencer. The separate knower, who is the finite limited being, shifts as the field of experiencing shifts, from being a mere separate subject to the aliveness of *What Is*. And yet the wonder is never lost.

You are so much more than you think

In the dance of separation the assumed knower is an object in experiencing, as is everything, absolutely everything—whether known or knowable. The one you call 'me' is a limited portal of experience, an open door into a precious playground, a finite expression exploring the world of objects: its ups and downs, pains and sorrows, joys and delights. Exploration occurs not through a separate self, the avatar, but as *Infinite Aliveness* itself.

You, and all objects, are vehicles of experiencing, and nothing less than the marvel of pure wonder.

That there is anything here at all is the true mystery. That you can experience life in all its many formations is beyond stunning. Words make beggars of the reality. Seeing *What Is*, what you are, stuns the chattering mind into silence.

The experience of the sweet human blips back and forth in life. One moment embedded in the sense of two, the next dipping into silent abidance, then back to separation, often without a scrap of recognition of the movement that never stops.

Are you looking for an escape ramp?

When we are consciously trying to figure life out and transform our ignorance, misinformation causes consternation and confusion. Misinformation: I've used that word previously, perhaps it is time that I flesh it out. There are many ways we are fed misinformation. We do it to ourselves, trusting what we think and feel, what we see and believe. We see what we think, and the thoughts that appear are based in what we have been programmed to believe. It's quite a maze of circles, round and round we go, finding proof for what we've been told. We don't see what doesn't fit even though it is right in front of us. What we see is the natural out-picturing of our inner process.

The appearances that seem to confirm our biases are but one type of misinformation. We also feed off the scraps of others' biases, friends and family and society at large.

We feast on the leavings of authority figures, teachers we trust, people whose opinions we value, and the ones who simply say something that catches hold within. Their offerings cannot but be based in their experiences that are inherently biased by the programs running within them. It is nearly impossible to eat from a clean table, one empty of misinformation.

That misinformation is the nub of duality's bad rap. Wanting something different, craving an escape, life itself is blamed. By the time the seeker has recognized the truth of who she is, that there is no way to figure it out, the blips simply blip, for the role of seeker has been fulfilled.

Life never abandons its dance, a dance that could only appear in duality, but life continuously calibrates the field of options, widening in embrace of everything, narrowing into nothing. Having brought the seeker feature to the choiceless choice—the one that could not help but be made—each new breath, every unresisted experience, opens into a more permanent union as the totality, as *Infinite Aliveness*.

Unraveling continues. It takes infinite shapes and forms, as innumerable as grains of sand on an endless beach. Each expression is unique. To tell you the specifics of my story would not help you: it would muddy your waters, giving you comparison points, new ways to judge yourself and others. It would also tell the story of a separate self who awakened and that would be a lie. It would reinforce the falsehoods that life strips away, the conditioned reality impersonating truth.

Making duality the bad guy misses the mark. You can't recognize the inseparable while cutting it into pieces: duality—bad, nonduality—good. This sections off the bits of you that don't make the cut in your more acceptable version of life.

That's separation, the concept, the idea of solidity, of materiality, performing on the personal stage.

Reality is far different from anything you can think, and is all-inclusive in ways you can't conceive until you experience the wonder, and then you can't do anything but laugh in awe. Oh ... good God ... that's what the mystics meant! I would have never guessed!

If you can think it, it's not it. Anything you can imagine is as far from the truth as believing the neighbor's 4-H pig sprouted wings and is flying overhead. Even the kids with a model rocket won't make Miss Piggy fly. NASA could, but that's cheating.

CHAPTER 20

Default Patterns

When you feel separate it means that there is a protective mechanism at play, a somatic default strategy that is adept at hide 'n seek. Because it is so very good at hiding, you can often only see it—or sense it—once much of your surface-level resistance is dealt with. Sometimes it manifests physically and sometimes just as an energetic presence. Once you see the beliefs, the thoughts, the physical body—the more compressed energy field—begins its deeper integration process. Seeing through the idea of separation is a new beginning for the body too.

Unknown to me, my bodily energy had mastered the trick of folding in upon itself. It was a way to be small, to stay off the radar screen of the world. It was a handy trick when life felt risky, when being seen seemed dangerous. Paradoxically what I really wanted, what I desperately needed was to be intimately seen, seen for the truth residing within, the love that I am. Too many disappointments, too many harsh words had taught the value of hiding, and driven it home with zeal.

Over the years, after doing all that inner work, who would have imagined that this default mode was still active. Until I saw it, I truly had no idea it was there.

How do you make yourself small?

When I noticed the pattern in myself, it was happening at the energetic level. It hadn't yet shown up in my physical appearance to any noticeable degree. Many of us develop a stoop over the years and seeing the precisely folded energy, it was easy to see one of the ways that may happen.

Seeing the pattern, I realized that I folded myself up, tipping the crown chakra energy down towards my little Buddha belly, wrapping my shoulders inward to seal off the gaps. Unknowingly, I built a bulwark against the form my life was taking. It was a default mechanism of the sense of separation, a protective attitude that wormed its way into protected status.

I was capable of abiding as awareness, but after a moment or more of simple experiencing, as not-twoness, I could feel the wide-open infinitely empty spaciousness, the *Infinite Aliveness* I am, begin to fold in upon itself.

Have you noticed your default yet?

Our natural reaction to *This* is to return to the known, to the familiarity of contraction, because the known, regardless of its level of discomfort, feels more comfortable than wide-open expansiveness. It doesn't make any sense at all since contraction is pretty unpleasant conditioning. Conditioning is the known, the familiar. It feels safer to go with that. It's less of a threat to the individuated body than unknown, naked experiencing.

Quite naturally, when threatened with infinite eternality, instinct commences a return to stasis, to reflex lifelessness. It is an entrenched movement away from the innate magnificence of *What Is*.

This habitual response—neither sound nor unsound in itself—was the instinctive way I programmed myself to care for my tender heart. Habits, especially body habits, don't generally disappear in the wink of an eye once the separate self is seen for what it is. They tend to hang around a bit. The habit is no longer needed or required, but the habituation still reacts, only with less certainty supporting it.

Waking up, noticing that what you truly are is awareness —and its entire contents—doesn't immediately call a ceasefire to the infolding, or at least it didn't in my case. This energetic system continued, but with one significant difference: instead of being fixated on my lines in the dream's script, I noticed the small shifts as they occurred.

Not as distracted by mind's weavings, you are quite capable of noticing anything that is out of alignment with the flow. Noticing, returning to basic experiencing, organically redirects the energy from the embedded fallacy to clearing out the misinformation.

Breaking open—like life—is often hard

It's often uncomfortable to allow the openness, to feel the tug-o-war, to notice it and let it be. The discomfort is frequently palpable as you watch the protective energy infolding; it can be quite difficult to stay with it, to allow it to continue. You aren't breaking the habit. The habit is being broken. Your experience, the magnificent *Infinite Aliveness* does it all.

The observing, the noticing, is the habit breaking. Infolding happens all the time unnoticed. If you can watch as it completes its arc, as it makes something of nothing, a guarded figurine enshrouded in a crystallized spell, you may wonder why humans would do that to themselves.

The answer is quite simple. Locking yourself down, going through the energetic contortions to close off your heart, feels safer than feeling what you are desperate to avoid. Through life's bumps and bruises, breaks and losses, you have learned that feeling life as it is will kill you, so it is a trade-off, one you are willing to make. The alternative feels much too risky. You are not consciously aware you are doing it, and at the time could do nothing else.

There's no one to blame

When your mother or father gave you *that look*, the one that unintentionally, or even intentionally, said that you were not good, that you were not loved, your little heart cracked, and then cracked again until it finally broke. Your beautiful little being felt so exposed, so tender and raw, that you feared letting anyone in, letting anyone come too close … so you infolded. You energetically tucked yourself in a dark room in its farthest corner, and crimped yourself tight into the fetal position. You went back to the womb, the closest you could get to home in a human body.

Infolding is part of the human condition. The path of self-protection only becomes more familiar after the first wounding of innocence. You did it so many times that you forgot how painful it felt until infolding was a natural response and you no longer noticed how much it hurt.

Over time it came to reflect your mostly unconscious view of life—painful and filled with suffering—and definitely something to avoid. Infolding could have been utterly gruesome—as it was, as it is—and you would still have done it. It wasn't premeditated. It wasn't even reasonable. It was instinctual.

The time it first occurred—and many times after—you believed you needed it to survive. Now the habitual is so normalized that you quit noticing it. Even when you are free mentally, the body still has a lot of energy invested in its story, the creased and crystallized patterns that will continue to run their familiar and often quite negative agenda.

How could energy ever be separated?

Everything is energy, the movement of aliveness taking form and releasing it, including your body and its wounds, its openness, and all apparent points in between. It is called many names: energy—consciousness—awareness—isness. All are words for simple, basic experiencing, experiencing that is unconditional, that does not preclude any experience.

Nothing could be excluded in the one that is not-two. It is not possible. There is nothing outside, no outside or in, no separate things, nothing to exclude, well, that is ... if you don't take *is* too seriously. It's a good functional word, but still a pointer.

The body unwinds as it will, as the personal field and the totality of experience, the infinite informational field of energy. There is no body separate from thought, no mind or body separate from world, no world separate from experience, no experience separate from the experiencer. What happens at any level happens at all levels—thought, body, world, experience. They are different appearances in experiencing but not separate.

What happens to you happens to me, happens to the world, whether you realize it, whether you feel it or not. When any crack in your accepted reality appears the entirety changes, and previously unseen possibilities are instantly within reach of all.

Every opening, every shadow that is integrated, every broken connection that is healed, heals the world.

Olly olly oxen free! Time to end the game of hide 'n seek

Once you see the infolding you may still infold but it can't hide any longer. The habit may not stop, or even slow down, but you notice the movement. The crack, the noticing, is unstoppable. It unavoidably makes its way to the foundation. It has always been in motion, even before the crack first appears. That is the nature of aliveness.

This amazing designless design that you are is robust and infinitely resilient. The unwinding happens naturally. As the ties that bind you are noticed, they begin to relax and the world around you cannot but shift. The manifestation pipeline empties and refills with its perfect mirror images, with its couldn't-be-otherwise reflections of grandeur, be it echoes of tight infoldment or of *Infinite Aliveness* in varying states of embodiment. Each new image adds to the depth and precision of the next.

The beauty of the scenic overlook on the ever-changing journey is that the one who cares, who doesn't have patience, who minds the discomfort, who worries that the world doesn't have much time left, has been seen for what it is—a mental construct, a useful tool to explore all life offers, the eternally transitioning out-picturing of the inner landscape, and so now the experience is vastly different.

CHAPTER 21

Dance of Polarities

Being contracted is neither the negative nor the positive pole of expansion. It's true that expansion is more amenable to greater expansion and contraction makes further contraction more likely, but they are not good and evil twins. Like tends to naturally engender like, as a human pregnancy delivers a human baby, not a salamander.

Our experience is what it is. It couldn't be otherwise, so making one pole right and the other wrong serves no purpose, and in fact is a bit of a troublemaker, piling judgment on top of life's already sufficient pain load.

You are not being graded as a winner or loser, whether you recognize experiencing for what it is, or you are absolutely certain of separation, or even if you proclaim the validity of imaginary points in between. Where you stand is not up to you. It is the purview of the burgeoning information field, life's dynamic blueprint.

Noticing the experiencing, regardless of contents and the implicit sensations and feelings, sets up the opportunity for expansion to assume the lead. Whether you will notice or not is already in your blueprint when the experience arises.

You are never the loser, nor are you the winner. Winners and losers are simply ideas in the mind of separation.

Wouldn't it be nice if life behaved the way you want ... or would it?

If expansion is the blueprint's impetus, the recognition of experiencing is more efficient than not noticing, but expansion is not the only game in town, nor is it free of detours. Some of us are not players on the field of expansion this time around. We may be here instead, to investigate the wounds of life.

Whatever track you appear to be on, you will venture off track time and again, coming back to the road only to leave again. Were life linear, a time-stamped phenomenon, it would be easier to see the tracks, but that's not the way this unpredictable, uncontrollable mystery works. Those that seem the farthest afield may have already lapped the pack. There is no way to know.

From the expansion view, reality is centered in the splendor of experience, the rich tapestry of life, rather than speculative hearsay. Clearly seeing *What Is* eliminates the belief in separation, the source of contraction, even though it may not alter one visible thing. Pain or sorrow, grief and sadness, are still experienced, and in the shadow of recognition are still felt, only without the cushion of speculation blunting the sharp edges. This is life after all.

Seeing the intemporality, the impermanence of all life, looking through unclouded eyes uses no energy on denial or resistance, so ideas and the felt sense of separation begin to fade. There is no need, no pull, no gravity to the old misunderstanding when life is simply lived as it appears. Without the personalized fabricated story there is little to nothing left to populate the data field with counterfeit images of separation.

There's no expansion without contraction

Contraction has its own magnificence, its own deep magic.

Hearsay and dreams create worlds. Based entirely on imagination, contraction shapes galaxies and black holes, builds bridges and blows them up, tightens the hatches down to protect its very personal story, and releases its tight grip to embrace what it loves. It is the rush of exploding anger, the release of adrenaline and endorphins when flight or fight kicks in, the worry disrupting the momentum of laughter, and the creativity that builds rocket ships to the stars.

There is no life without contraction. Contraction is not a stepchild of expansion, not a lesser part of this grand experience. Its story is one of polarities, the drama of winning and losing, the comedy of foolishness and fantasy, the romance of beloveds, of family loved and tossed, of family loved and lost. It is the realm of heartache and heartbreak, of scrambling to survive and wondering why, of staying alive while wishing to die, while wishing for life to be over and done, and yet something about living keeps you holding on. That alone, even without the opportunity to see what makes it tick, to poke around the invisible heart of awareness, makes a human life worth incarnating for.

As you can see, duality is damn attractive.

Searching for truth or hunting for gold—it's all part of the dream

Just because the focus of your spyglass is set to find the wizard behind the curtain, it doesn't mean that it's the right or best setting. It's one of infinite possibilities. Holding any belief—even the belief in the holy importance of recognizing what's real—suspends recognition. Anything we know cuts us off from the unknown, and this *we are* is beyond knowing. It can be experienced but not known. A paradox for sure.

When we experience life's myriad possibilities from the contracted state we are not fully alive. We embody renunciation in our denial of the depth and breadth life offers, releasing but a sliver of its potential. It is a symphony only partially heard, listened to with ears alone. We forfeit the soul-touching mystery. There is so much more to experience when we start to let go of our natural inclination towards resistance and embrace new possibilities ... and this occurs as life wills it, when experiencing has broken through our defenses.

Aliveness is the open vulnerable heart, open to all possibilities. It is the willingness to feel instead of shutting down whatever there is to feel. It is all those things we were told were weaknesses. It is not looking away from life as it is. It is staring into the guts of pain, the eyes of the heartless, the still bleeding wounds. It says: *This too, just this, only this.* It is Christ on the cross, arms open wide, unmoving in embrace of this simple moment, of what's here now.

Yes is the only word you need

Aliveness has no need of control mechanisms, to be constrained by what is 'better'—what's seemingly more aligned with your particular version of spirituality. It simply opens in an infinite *yes, yes* to expanding horizons, and *yes* to anything that tries to suppress the insuppressible. When life's twists throw you off the narrow ledge, when it shoots off in an unexpected direction, even if that direction includes death and dying, when it upends your world with the smaller deaths of financial ruin or finding yourself sad and alone, aliveness stares life in the face and says: *Wow! I didn't expect that. Well ... here I am, all-inclusive me, tears and breaking heart included.*

Contraction is a hard *no* to life as it is. It resists what is appearing right now, right here. Even though it tries to alter life's course, it cannot change the unfolding mystery one whit, except perhaps by trying to ensure that life continues in the same unwanted direction, creating more contraction in its wake.

Contraction solidifies the dream, branding it *something to be avoided,* creating another monster under the bed. With each movement, contracted or expanded, intelligence is added to the field.

Adding constricted data points simply ensures that life will present more experiences to resist.

Expansion says: *Yes, hell yes!* The outer experience may reflect the same world as that of the resister, but the inner world is quite different. Manifestation's pipeline is no longer plugged up with false identities so aliveness manifests as it will. Naked of separation infatuations this *That Is* manifests without distortion, but not necessarily as a separate self might wish. Fortunately, that phantom is no longer in a position to take exception.

ACTUALITY

Contraction and expansion are neither valid nor flawed. They are differing, contrasting experiences, the delicate balance of the interactive display, the organic out-picturing of the faultless blueprint. In truth, aliveness is the only reality. It is the reality informing contraction and expansion, and gently, forcefully, inevitably, walking all of itself home.

One human lifetime, the all-inclusive expression of the entire spectrum, is a blip on the EKG monitor screen of infinity, and yet an exquisitely perfect blip, for it is the *All That Is* imbued with the fascinating idea that there is something other.

CHAPTER 22

Dream a Little Dream

You wake up. You see what's real, and still you can't escape the dream. You *are* the dream, the entirety of it. The dream of escaping fits in the category of flying pigs, just like the dream of annihilating a separate self. This universe, the cosmos, all the dimensions people talk about escaping to, that they hope to evolve or ascend into, are dreamland, the very real mirage, illusions of reality.

Is there a heaven or a hell? A fifth dimension? Is there an earth and a sky? A human who goes by your name? All appearances come from the same tree and are blossoms of the illusion of time and space, of self and other—the dream. In the dream any experience is possible.

Experiencing something, anything, means you are in the dream. The dream is not bad or inferior in any way. The dream is the experiencing wing of *this you are*. The dream is the known, the sensations that you feel, the exploits that tickle your fancy and strike you with terror, the connections that bring tears to your eyes and warmth to your heart.

In the dream, time appears to split the eternal now into past and present. Space, the infinite seen through the lens of individuation, gives the impression of something other than here, of distance, of a there. The illusion of time and space, when applied to thought, rolls out more illusions: continuity, thinking, a doer. The accepted deception creates links where there are none, and is the finite experience of separation.

So it's a dream—is that all bad?

When you are asleep, even if you are lucid, you are in the dream. When you are awake, even if you've noticed what this is, you are lucid within the waking dream. You have not escaped the dream. You are still in it. It is truly turtles all the way down[1]. There is nothing knowable that is not the dream.

To know something, to know anything, there must be a knower, a dreamer, the dreamed character. Does awareness know? Awareness is simply aware. Infinite being cannot experience life without the characters upon its world stage.

You are the sensing-feeling-body, *Infinite Aliveness* made manifest. The part, in this case the sensing-feeling-body, is no less infinite than the whole. Absent the body, *Infinite Aliveness* is pure potential without the means to experience itself, the life-blood without a heart. You are the heart of *Aliveness*. Sensations are not separate from the body, nor is the body separate from *Infinite Aliveness*. Even though they seem to be divisible, they are not. They are not-two.

This is not just a transcendental, ephemeral idea. Even in the materialist model, your DNA holds within it the code of

---

1. "Turtles all the way down" is an expression of infinite regress. The saying is based on the Native American legend of a World Turtle supporting a flat Earth on its back. The myth states that the turtle rests on the back of an even larger turtle, which itself is part of a column of increasingly larger turtles that continues indefinitely.

every protein in the body. Let that understanding ripple ... what is true at one level, is true at all levels. Just as your DNA holds the blueprint for your entire body, within you is life's DNA. You are the father and mother, the divine masculine and sacred feminine masquerading as the child.

What a fabulous bargain of a lifetime!

Awareness experiences life through countless filters. Awareness—unfiltered experiencing—and life, are not-two. Look with an innocent heart and you will see that the known arises in experiencing, displays itself as experiencing, returns into experiencing. There is nothing—known or knowable—that is other than simple, ever so basic, experiencing.

You can see for yourself. It truly isn't very difficult. It is so obvious that you look right past it. The human mind seems to need complexity and can only see what it is ready to see. You see what you believe you will see. Beliefs filter all sensory input. To see beyond your self-imposed limitations, to see the obvious, what actually is, unfiltered by beliefs, life pours uncertainty into what you think you know.

Diluting beliefs can be challenging, an understatement for certain, especially when they are diluted out of existence. It was difficult for me, perhaps because I held on with a tight fist. Even once I could see that all my beliefs had to go, that holding on didn't only cause suffering, but was suffering, I held on. Does it have to be that way? I don't know. I only know how it was here. That's all anyone can say.

In what ways are you hanging on?

Being stripped of my beliefs took more than even my wicked imagination could conjure. It took nearly dying, having the illusion of control ripped from my hands before I finally let go. The mind in my dreamworld was tenacious. As soon as one belief crumbled, and its shattered bits lay scattered on the floor, new ones took its place. My analytical tendency was to replace the existing belief with another: if x is not right, then y must be ... no, not so! I didn't have it in me to watch a belief disintegrate and leave the void untouched. Beliefs are the way we unconsciously hang onto the believer. You might swear you are ready and willing, praying to be delivered from the curse of separation, but if all the experiences necessary to undo the knot of separation have not occurred, your pleas will seemingly go unanswered.

And yet, the pleas, the prayers and supplications, the heart-wrenching screams in the middle of the night, the raised fist cursing the darkness, all the tears and anguish are the answer, are the eternally unfolding revelation playing out as your experience.

Whatever your experience, even given the countless variables, it is the exact and only expression that could be in this moment. It is the unwinding, unraveling, decompressing, magnificence of experiencing, of *This That Is*, expressing through the portal of your beautifully illusory heart, mind, and body.

Once the dream is seen to be the dream, the dream goes on, the dreamed character knows he is dreamed, is part of the wondrous cosmic notion. The need to escape, a story in the dream no longer holds sway, just like a nighttime dream of being chased by ghosts.

The ghost and the chase continue if that is part of the dreamland experience, fully experienced, met directly, tended carefully. Nighttime, daytime, asleep, awake, all is seen to be *Infinite Aliveness* in motion.

CHAPTER 23

The End of the Endgame

Truth is a loaded word. The idea of truth, or what most take to be truth, has its basis in duality. In duality, as soon as one thing is true, something else is automatically false. Black must have its white. Truth lives in the domain of a separate self who has a need to know, a desire to find The Truth, who wants to be the one to grab the carousel's brass ring.

What we perceive as true through eyes fixed in duality is not exactly false; but it is limited to its associated degree of understanding. Through that lens, the appearance is real—separate, stand-alone, material, solid. It is what it seems to be.

In *Actuality*, the appearance is real. Surprised? It's an intricate, intimately real illusion, a seemingly solid reality. Within an illusion, anything can be real … nothing can be real … both polarities can be real at the same time. *Actuality* (as foolhardy as it is to set down in print) can be experienced but it is challenging to communicate. It organically posits the possibility of opposites being true, as true as any idea or concept can be since everything that can be conceived is experienced as relative. Simultaneously, it posits the opposite, the reality that nothing is definitively true. It is all-inclusive, real and not real, solid and not solid, here and not here, mystical and physical without a bit of separation while including the illusion of separation.

Is there such a thing as truth?

Any truth or falsehood that can be imagined is by its very nature, qualified. It is limited to the imagination in which it arises, which certainly complicates the discovery a bit. It is, though, important to understand that what the conditioning sees as true is not on the same planet, let alone cosmos, as *Infinite Aliveness*. What's imagined to be true and what is actually present here-now are light years apart.

Discovering what's here is not about becoming enlightened or shifting, changing, developing, evolving—period. It's not about knowing something that will positively affect manifestation or change the contents of experience, although that's the incentive early on the path. Along the way you realize that the initial goal will not be achieved, and there never was an endgame after all.

The journey of discovery is about noticing what, if anything, is real. It is about not living in the false, as a character in the story of life, but living as life itself.

If you are looking for a better life, noticing what is true may alter the shape and form of the experience instantaneously, or appear to have little or no effect. It does, however, alter the flavor and texture of the experience. When you see what life is, what you are, resistance to its appearances falls away, and fighting what's happening feels insane. You stop minding what's appearing, so without the battle—the argument with life—the experience of it cannot but change. As to the content of experience, as you've heard here repeatedly, it might shift, then again it might not. The mind doesn't want to accept that. The fight for something better is its job security.

Letting go of the dream ... from within the dream

What! No life improvement? It's a good thing that *you* aren't doing it, that you don't have a choice, because without the assumed bonus at the end, few would knowingly take more than a few steps down this road. Letting it go, releasing the self-focus, is the attribute of experiencing and its *See the Truth and Be Set Free* feature.

Being aware of the dreamlike nature of life changes the dreamer. When you awaken from a dream you know it was not real. The enchantments—the monsters, angels and stand-ins—lacked any substance whatsoever. Sometimes, the dream feels so real that it seems to permeate the non-sleeping state for a while. You may even reach out to the person you dreamt about to reassure yourself it wasn't a premonition of something real to come.

That type of dream is close to the surface, as real as anything in the waking state. It is a pointer to the unreality of all dreams, waking and asleep, but instead of seeing it for what it is, you quite naturally attempt to box it in, hiding it in the tidy storage container of labels and acceptable answers.

The box is a lion tamer, taming those experiences that don't fit neatly into your story about life, your understanding of what this is, and who you are. You tame the misfits, the mystical, magical, unexplainable happenings, beseeching them to behave, using your misunderstanding of the waking state as your template. You innocently overlay fabrication onto what is already fabricated, piling false onto false. That is the nature of the counterfeit reality's spell.

Do you question the givens in your life?

It has worked for generations, and rarely has it been questioned. It reinforces the carefully constructed sense of safety, rationalizing the orchestrated mortal reality, the Sleeping Beauty enchantments, until it's easy to slip back into the dream, free of anything unnerving to disrupt your slumber.

A powerful sense of the material world goes hand in hand with a reinforced sense of separateness, of 'me-ness'. Firmly entrenched in your rationalization, you experience a material world of sensation, perception, thought, and emotion and yourself as a material girl or boy. But this isn't how it is; the world and everything known isn't material; it is a fleshed-out story taking center stage in holo-land and you have a starring role in this exquisitely real hologram, this very real mirage, this magically real dream. Why argue with that?

You either live as if the dream is a material reality or awaken within the dream. The recognition of *What Is*, the nature of your nature, while capable of altering any experience, placing it in alignment with the living *Actuality*, is quite capable of turning manifestation on its head.

The depth of realization necessary to set habitual patterns free could instantly manifest in aligned perfection, but residual unwillingness to see, to recognize *What Is* and drop the facade, coupled with the stranglehold on what you believe you know, almost ensures the re-creation of those same patterns.

What if comfort is overrated?

You are attuned to the habitual myth of materiality. The habitual is ingrained in everything you do, everything you are, all the ways you view the world. It is so ingrained, not just in you, but in humanity, that you do not see it at all until it pushes up against your new recognition in uncomfortable ways. Embrace the discomfort. It is grace in action, unearthing those parts of you still resonating with the old story.

When you recognize the dream for what it is, you do not have to overcome the enchantments. They dissolve as they will and when they will... or not at all. Seen for what they are, the dream remains, but you know it is a dream.

The dreamed character continues her dream walk. The traumas within the dream, the traumas of life are felt, deeply utterly painstakingly, and because they are not resisted, they do not burrow in and find a forever home. They move on as they will, for everything is in motion when you meet it directly.

Not wanting to feel, not being able to meet experience as it unfolds before you, within you, *as* you, will divert the flow, delaying the momentum, crystalizing the energy. Sometimes it's conscious; most often it's not. You automatically push back because you put your faith in the dream. When you see that life is the dream—the big dreaming—that there is no harm, no lasting forever harm, and you are a dreamed character without input into a dreamed story, a story that includes the appearance of choice, there is nothing left to push against. Whether each experience slips away slowly, or with lightning quickness, no longer matters.

If the world were really a dream—would it be so bad?

The work, the undoing unraveling unfolding, is life. You might say: *Why bother?* But the answer is that you cannot not. Whatever shape and form life takes is the work … or the play, is the unfolding, the sparkling aliveness, the not so hidden treasure.

Now that I see through the smoke and mirrors, life opens into a goldmine whose bottom I have yet to find. I seriously doubt there is a bottom. There could be. I leave that open, as with all appearances, but finding the bottom is like saying life itself could end. This expression could dissolve into nothingness, but *life* ending—absurd. *This* is life. There is nothing but life. Experiencing, and the multiplicity of its expressions, is life. How could that end?

We are not material objects in a material world. That is undoubtedly the experience, the appearance, and it is not nothing. It is precious beyond words.

This illusory world is the awakening playground, the divine experiential, the doorway through which infinite being experiences itself, expands itself, feels itself, discovers itself.

Just because it's a dream doesn't make life less appealing

The world is not a by-product, a lesser, measly subordinate. It is life itself, equally priceless, equally infinite and eternal. It is the movement of the non-moving, the phantasmagorical display of the kaleidoscope of awareness, the finite presence of the infinite. It is to be celebrated.

The living vibrant dynamic field of experiencing is love at its basis, love that is not transactional, that is not what we think of as love at all.

It is absolute surrender to life, succumbing to love and its wily ways.

It is quite natural to default to old behaviors, but the pain of dissonance triggers the reminder, bringing you back into alignment—by design. The quest for anything beyond this moment, anything other than life as it is, points to remnants of the old belief still twisting in the wind of a separate self. The quest grants its object a temporary separation dispensation from *Infinite Aliveness*. Your assured return to unshackled aliveness reveals that there never was a need to quest and no one to don the valiant knight's armor.

Whether the body displays that truth or not is irrelevant. The body, like every little thing, is the dream, an appearance in experiencing. While the dream does as it does, the lack of outer perfection is not a judgment, an accusatory statement about your level of realization ... or anyone else's. This world and its players are so much more than one expression's remembrance. There is not-two. The inner expresses as the outer. Until every variable resonates in aliveness there is always more to unravel ... and even then, there is no end.

CHAPTER 24

The Hope of Awakening

As hope for an improved life lets go, it is still common to believe that there is still a goal, a jackpot, the perfection you have searched for your entire life—in other words, *awakening*. If it's not to be found on the material level, then it must be available on the spiritual. It is not an unusual belief … and surprisingly true, but not in the ways you might think.

Awakening is a misused and misunderstood word. It might be better to toss it in the firepit and cheer as it turns to ash.

What we call 'awakening' is but a step on an infinite ladder, the first rung in a journey that actualizes the recognition, bringing it to ground, stripping the fallacies bare. It is the end of the search for the human avatar, but thank goodness, not the end of its journey of discovery.

Most of us are asleep in the backseat, caught in the dream, and momentarily satiated by glimmers of escape. We still want the pretty things for our human—control, a better life, a more humane world, understanding, respect, community—and if we can't have them, or finally see that's not what this is all about, we pull the magical switcheroo and settle for a way out.

Awakening is one of many possible escape routes.

Awakening is deemed the golden toy in ascension's toybox. Paradoxically it's an idea that belongs to materiality, as all ideas do. It's popular because life feels prettier when painted with the colors of awakening—the grandest of grand escapes that promises darkness will turn to light, the shadows will slip back into the cracks, and you will rise above this plane, a blossoming lotus where a weed once grew.

Judgment: a good indicator that you are still on the wheel

When you have this preconception, you don't accept that many of the seemingly independent individuals who have recognized what reality is, have actually done so. They are just too human. You also deny that recognition for yourself. You compare what *is* here with your story of what *should* be and think that they, and you, are missing something, that you have yet to arrive, that you couldn't have recognized what you are. You say to yourself that awakening just couldn't look like that. Your boxed-up ideas about the look and feel of self-recognition, and how awakened beings should act, keep you skipping over the obvious, overlooked, way too simple, could-not-be-that reality of awakening.

What? All those quirks don't go; they aren't annihilated? Life's mixed bag isn't replaced with abundance and beauty? Wait!

Waking up leaves the human foibles and personality intact? Good lord! That means the golden toy can't be that golden …

The fantasy alleges that, after an awakening event of

mythic portent, the damaged, wounded self magically mystically becomes unbroken, spotless, pristine. It's a surprisingly good fantasy. It's so appealing that it is packaged differently across the planet—*ascension, awakening, the rapture, heaven, the black void*. Same, same, just a bit different, each heralds the ultimate escape from life's pain.

If only it were true.

Would you really want that ultimate escape?

No. Wait! You don't want it to be true, for if it were … oh my, how the stars shudder at the thought. That would open Pandora's box, releasing the great blasphemy that there is two: the pain and the escape route; incomplete omniscience, finite omnipresence, emasculated omnipotence; limits on the limitless, boundaries in boundlessness; seams, breaks, beginnings, and endings; a separate self who awakens.

Isn't that the whole idea behind Satan, the one who set himself apart from God? What a misunderstood, and yet divinely inspired pointer.

The misunderstanding, misrepresentation, miscalculation of an awakened being could only be accurate if it is indeed the separate self that wakes up, if there actually is a separate self that could awaken, if awareness is not sufficiently aware, sufficiently indivisible that division could occur. If that were the case the judgy constraints used to abuse ourselves and others would make sense, would be the way life actually is. With that shift in the story, so would wars, poverty, and hate for they are all structures built upon the same misunderstanding.

Phew! Dodged that bullet!

Fortunately, the fantasy is merely a fantasy, the story another story made up by stringing together a collection of escape thoughts. When belief in separation loses its ability to persuade, what remains is what was always present—mysterious beauty, precious aliveness, the dance of the infinite. Were the separation story true, none of that would be imaginable, let alone possible to experience.

Noticing what you are leaves dreamland untouched, for dreamland is the endless expression of the expression-less, not something your realization wipes out. The dream continues. You don't recognize you are solely the expression-less—that's the escape hatch. You recognize you are the totality—the expression, and that in which it arises: the expression-less—the father-mother and the child.

That recognition instantly alters the experience of the illusory dream—even though that instant may slowly unfold, slow motion trainwreck-slow, revealing itself over years or lifetimes—but when the illusion finally pops, when you are steeped back into this *you are*, no doubt remains, no way back into the solid character can be found. There is no return to your old tightly held, completely harebrained beliefs. All need to search drops like a ripe pear in autumn.

You are filled with relief, but what has changed?

Habituated appearances stop by for a visit now and again, but they don't have the zing they used to, the staying power, the ability to influence, to convince. It seems that the held energy in the body tends to leak out slowly. The resistance, though, is gone like air from a balloon pricked with a sharp pin.

And then, life begins.

Your experience cannot determine the level of your awakened being. There are no levels. Levels are part of the dream of separation. There. Are. No. Levels.

Although, for most, it appears that we shed separation much more slowly than a remedial snake shedding its skin, and just as progressively. It appears that we learn, grow, and evolve in a linear fashion, ploddingly releasing our stories. All of that is set firmly within the dream, the dream of levels and expansion, of surrender and resistance, of attachment and aversion. In the dream is in the dream ... and we're all in the dream. It is the story of waking up, alas a story, nonetheless.

Everything *is*; nothing is not

Does the appearance of leveling up lead to awakening? Heck yes! But then again everything does. That's what the dream is, a working dream. This *you are* is reeling itself back in from the moment it pops out of the womb of life as you, the moment the infinite takes on finite form. Aliveness is the ultimate fly fisherman casting a line made of fractalized light.

Incarnated, you have access to limitless experiences. You, the unbound, are the character experiencing the bound. You are a divinely ephemeral, ordinarily earthy part of the dream, regardless of the dream's content. It could be a dream of riches and power, or a dream of awakening. In every case it is still the dream. Anything known is the dream, including these words you are reading.

That's a real disappointment for some, but to those who see clearly it is freedom. There is no escaping the dream.

There is the dream, and misunderstanding, disregarding, or recognizing the reality of the dream.

You both are, and are not, the dream character. *This* is nothing you can imagine.

You do not just see through your character's eyes, experience your character's perceptions and sensations; you are self-aware *Isness* having a human life, experiencing itself in form. This *you are* is *Infinite Aliveness*, your human avatar, and *All That Is*, not either one or the other, not becoming or forsaking, but *both*, all, the infinite multiplicity of expressions simultaneously.

You are so much more than whatever you believe ...

This incarnation is not separate from what you are. There is not-two. Whenever there is trouble you can be sure that the idea of two is lurking in the shadows, and you've forgotten that the visible expression of the expressionless is not a lesser substitute. It is the celebration of *Isness*, the holy display of life.

Experiences, and the idea of an experiencer, appear and disappear in this *you are*. It does not matter to experiencing what appears within it. Experiencing doesn't care whether there seems to be an experiencer or not. It does not notice that everything experienced is only experienced here: here in the center point, in nowness illuminated through the portal of light and shadow. It does not mind if the experience is one of relationship or aloneness, of abundance or abject poverty, of happiness and peace or deep inconsolable grief. Experiencing does not know that it is allness, *Infinite Aliveness*, the play of awareness, and all of which it is aware. Experiencing simply *is*.

Despise your human condition if you must. Self-flagellation has its role too. Contrast is valuable. Eventually you will come back around to awe, sweet *aaaah!* That is the built-in default of your brilliant nature. One day soon, you will drop to your knees and beg your precious human's forgiveness. *Oh, sweet little one, I am so sorry. Every time I said no to you, to your experience, I was spinning in imagination. There was never anything to resist, anything that needed to change. You were always perfect as you are.*

May soon be soon ... although in a timeless world, who cares?

CHAPTER 25

Does Love Always Win?

Love always wins is a common hope, cloaked in the form of solid belief amongst spiritual folk: It's easy to see why people believe it. Who wouldn't want it to be true? It is a widespread ideology, not evidence of proof, and many of us ignore the role of that ideology in giving us a reason to bypass our deep shadow work.

Believed or not, the question remains. Does love always win?

Through the many lenses of duality it doesn't seem like love always wins. It doesn't even *feel* like love always wins. Ideologies aside, does it? Is the cliche true? Does love win in the long run? If yes, how long a run? In my lifetime? In the lifetime of my children or grandchildren? In the next 200,000 years?

What exactly does love always wins mean?

What is your sense of this? Does love always win?

Believing that love wins is used as an excuse to sit back and wait for it to triumph, a reason given to let resistance go untended, to watch as love overcomes the challenges of life while you are tucked in with your habits, your unfinished business, and the comfort of your tried-and-true world.

It is a love and light mantra used to justify the means. Anything goes because love will always win. Setting the potential for damage aside, it still begs a couple of questions: whose version of love, and who gets to decide what winning looks like?

All ideologies that are held to be true stand in the way of clear seeing, of recognizing what this actually is, because all understanding rooted in separation—which is basically all understanding—is a misrepresentation of reality.

What do you mean by love?

Back to the question. Are we talking about a separation variant of love or what's real? More specifically, if love wins, what does winning mean in a dream; how can the self that is not separate win, and against whom; and if there is winning to be done, what does war look like between the one that is not-two?

You are made of love. There is nothing but love when you define love as *Infinite Aliveness*, and I have yet to find a better definition. How could that win or lose?

An old friend and I used to describe life as being made up of *hearticles*, a little play on particles. What's fascinating is that she is an old friend, not a current friend. We traversed the infinite field of aliveness together for years and still, at least in human form, love didn't appear to win. We could not hold the friendship together. Life undid us.

The breakup of our relationship was part of the great unfolding, exposing traumas still hiding in creases inside the folds. It led me into the hidden shadows of abandonment, the sense of aloneness, the deep hold-out fold of betrayal, and being forever misunderstood and unforgiven. What it offered her I do not know, although I am certain her path was no easier than mine.

On my journey, I came to a place where I didn't care if we were disconnected before I came to forgiveness. I tried so many times to fix us that I finally just gave up. Having reached the fertile ground of futility, I had nothing left to give. Forgiveness, the idea of forgiving us, took last place. I knew, I still know, that she is not simply she, and I am not simply I, that we are this *Infinite Aliveness* and its forms, but still the energy of forgiveness needed to cycle through, to work its magic in the clearing field.

When life seems unfathomable your feelings will tell you what you need

Unlike most other fields of forgiveness I had wandered, I didn't blame myself for our separation. I simply didn't understand how or why it happened. I didn't assign or take personal blame. I just felt hurt. The abandonment energy ran strong, but as in all things, I couldn't see what I couldn't yet see.

I had lost so many important people in my life—my beloved husband, my mother, my best friend, all to death in a very small window of time. To lose another beloved broke me, but I couldn't wear the cloak of brokenness for long. I couldn't do that to myself again. I had nothing left for grief, so instead, and without realizing it, I took on the mantle of indifference.

Being broken was a gift. The breaking ripped our shared world apart, leaving me standing on my own, tearing me away from the last person with influence over me, an essential friend whose words could make me doubt my experience.

I stepped away from a teacher some years before and lost my community, the many trusted souls I relied upon, and this relationship had a similar feel, although that was not intentional, nor was it nearly as dominating. I had grown and changed, but not enough to see through the distorted ideas of personal intent and domination. In my unwillingness to prod the dysfunction out into the open, I apparently was willing to let it all ride. My complacency, my hesitance to confront the self-abandonment, sparked a complete reset, sending our worlds spinning in different directions.

Your brokenness wants to be seen

It would have been so much easier if I had been able to see my latent tendencies and lay them on the table without resistance or, barring that, if I could have walked away without needing to be torn apart. It doesn't seem to happen with ease very often. It seems to require a reboot of some sort and that reboot is usually painful.

After a while, the brokenness could not be contained, would not stay where I had stuffed it down out of sight. That's the beauty of brokenness. It wants to be seen, to be felt, to heal itself, to whole itself. That's the discomfort you feel in your body, the brokenness trying to rise to the surface and your mostly unconscious effort to push it back down into the depths.

There is a constant battle—a war within—between wholeness and its shattered pieces. The pieces are magnetized to the pull of their whole design and cannot leave you to your brokenness, no matter how well you hide them.

They are always wiggling free, floating to the surface, willing you to feel them, to free them and yourself.

So yes, in that sense, love always wins. Life will always point you back to love. The hard lessons will bestow opportunities to love the ever-new moment more completely, to free the trapped energy of fear and anger, hatred and harm, trauma and despair that are hidden within by your innocent inability to feel what seems to be terminal brokenness, irretrievable wholeness.

If you recognized *what you are*, would winning or losing matter?

When love wins does it look like heaven on earth? Does it mean the world will heal and return to wholeness? Will hate disappear? Will peace and happiness reign?

In a world of duality, of knower and known, that is impossible. The dichotomy is the very nature of separation, of the fall from grace. Is it possible for all separation to end, for every sentient being to see through the maze of individuality? Anything is possible, and yet, you will have to wait and see, for any supposition puts you back in the maze, in time, in separation, the Gordian knot revisited.

And ... when you know who you are, when you remember what this is, you don't have to wait. It is already heaven on earth regardless of the contents of the dream. Love has already won.

There was never a war or battle for love to lose. There never was nor could there ever be a separate anything or anyone to war against.

ACTUALITY

To live that reality, to let it all the way in to the center of your body, your mind and your psyche, heart splayed open in full surrender, to move through the shadow of death, and know beyond the shadow of doubt that experience is the dream arising in and as the innate aliveness, now that is a big win for love.

CHAPTER 26

Resisting Resistance

While resistance makes life more painful and seeing what is actual more difficult, it is not an invalid experience. At one time I thought it was. Everyone said it was *the* big mistake, the behavior in need of correction. There is no mistake. Life doesn't make mistakes. Mistakes are an idea in separation.

Resistance is the energy at the core of a separate self. Without resistance there is no separation. And yet, neither the separate self nor the resistance that appears to create it is a problem. How could something made entirely of thought be an actual factual problem?

Resistance is an experience and experiencing is the beloved jewel. *This That Is* reveals itself both *in* and *as* experiencing, so resistance is a revelatory pointer, not a problem. Resistance is thought taken seriously, an idea concretized as hardened belief. Thought also arises in and as experiencing. It is not a problem either. It, like all of life, is the mirror revealing the existing conditions.

The sense of resistance appears as a thought in what you call 'mind'. As you will know, if you've explored this, mind doesn't actually exist, it is not substantive. Mind *seems* to be the thinker, or at least belong to a thinker, but is nothing but threaded thoughts. All things—thoughts, mind, thinker, resistance—appear to be objects known by a subject (you)—that's the nature of the grand simulation—but they are basic experiencing, not subject, not objects. They are that which appears to be two but is not.

... and we've circled back around to experiencing

If you've looked, you have seen that it is impossible to separate experience from the experiencer. If you stopped and made yourself available to your experience, you saw that this is not veiled, it is not hidden and there's no need for a big reveal. While *Actuality* is not difficult to see, letting it rewrite all that you thought you knew presents more of a challenge. Seeing through the fallacy is quick and easy in comparison.

We humans tend to be very much attached to our separate world experience. The fallacy is indelibly inscribed on mind and body. The basics alone (this is a physical world; we have a material body) may take the rest of our lives to unravel fully, and there is plenty more to unwind beyond the basics. Once the recognition of what this is occurs, it slowly reverberates throughout the entire body-mind mechanism. Before the recognition, life's unraveling is like trudging through wet concrete. Afterwards, it's a walk on a smooth sidewalk—well, smooth*er* might be more accurate.

You are an orb of experiencing aware of your own little world. You don't see what you are because of your certainty. You were raised to know. Family, and your community, gave you their answers, and their truths were not truths. You were presented with a materialist world, a determinate nature of reality, so unwittingly you resist *What Is* and bow down to what is not. Even ideas of God are based in duality—God and you, heaven and earth, angels and devils.

An intellectual, mind-only understanding is but the beginning ...

It's not that hard to get this intellectually, but getting it all the way in, so far in that your automatic default resets, requires an ever-deepening dive, which life is quite happy to oblige.

You resist even though you have seen what is true. Resistance is your inheritance in a material world. It is mindlessly habitual, an argument with reality that pushes back against your experience as it is. It is your refusal to consider that your experience is not what you believe it is, in your socially indoctrinated and personally enforced wisdom. It is the belief that you know what other people are talking about, that you understand the meaning of their words, that you grok the experience they cannot even put into words. It is the concept *I*, the belief in a self, the dissonant reality you blindly trust that does not exist as you think.

Resistance is believing you know what stuff is—life, the body, a world, dimensions, death—the stuff filling up the contents of your experience. Thinking the physical is reality is a solid deterrent to seeing what actually is, even when you add a spiritual element. *Knowing* turns your experience into something finite, limited and solid. It also disguises the inherent inflexibility, disconnection and contraction, making it seems like you are embracing life.

That *seeming* fogs up the mirror ...

It's akin to standing inside a thick concrete tube with a lightning rod on top. The lightning storm cannot strike you and you feel secure—mostly. You are still breathing, protected from the storm, experiencing a version of life inside the tube, a version you think is the real deal, but you are not fully alive. You may be safe, but you are cut off from the changing weather that is *Infinite Aliveness*.

The experiences of inflexibility, disconnection and contraction are just as much what you are as openness, connectivity and joy. It is more difficult to admit to 'negative' experiences, but they are not something to avoid.

They are the cattle prods of experience, creating uncomfortable sensations that require you to look deeper.

When you are happy and at peace there is little incentive to let go of the indoctrination. It works for you, life seems good and there's no need for change. That's why pain and suffering, the stepchildren of resistance, are so powerful and important. They are openings to new possibilities, the opposite of a comfortable indoctrinated approach to living.

So, if you inquire into the disconnection that flows out of resistance—if you inquire with genuine, almost childlike, interest, it will annul the indoctrination and the misdirection that comes from a self-protective, misinformed world. All experiences, even resistance, hold within them their undoing.

Are you genuinely willing to explore your beliefs in a material world?

It is closer to say that life is an indescribable dynamism of light, or miraculous explosions of energy, than to call this a material world. This is pure potential temporarily assuming the form of perceptions sensations thoughts emotions

–*Presence* presencing—eternally on full display in infinite patterns shapes colors textures. You are not a mortal; you are a majestic, breathtakingly beautiful prismatic effusion of aliveness that excludes nothing, not even resistance. In your knowing you miss the show, the delights of fractalized light, the magic of this you are reflected back to you.

Resistance cannot stop the unbuttoned-up display of *What Is*. It cannot dampen the aliveness or the experience of that aliveness, even when the experience feels like a contracted mess. It may harden your resolve, your belief in your convictions, the conviction in your beliefs. It may even make you turn your head and heart from what you resist, but that is an experience—the experience of turning away—and that too, is *This*.

As important as recognizing who you are is the realization of what experience really is. They are identical twin inquiries and both reveal the same thing. You cannot understand experience if you do not recognize the truth of the experiencer, and you cannot truly grasp experience when you hold outdated beliefs about the reality of experience that were never true. Experience when innocently delved into, when seen for what it is, tasted sensed felt directly, takes you to the realization of the fabric of experience and experiencer, fabric being as good a word as any, for there are no words that come close.

It won't feel safe. Safety is an idea composed of threaded thoughts ...

Seeing that you are awareness may leave traces of separation intact, an experiencer and the contents of experiencing, a separate self in a new spiritual robe waiting to be annihilated. Seeing what experience actually is takes care of that little blip.

It's pretty funny to see how creative the holographic human is. It will make up a new story to fit the changing evidence and tie it right back to the story that was just demolished, propping it up, dressing the naked emperor in new finery. Belief-ending experiences go against the grain, and experiencing the identity associated with them dissolve isn't at all comfortable.

Resistance is an identity; it *is* the identity. Without it, no separate self remains. Resistance requires something to resist, so for a time, recognizing the falsity of beliefs may create more subtle resistance. This is quite usual, until resistance has run its course all the way down to the last defendable straw.

That last straw is seeing clearly what experience is. This demolishes the emperor, the clothes and the whole wardrobe. Gone is any ability to rewrite the story, to tweak the evidence in the separate self's favor, to deny and decry the truth staring back at you, to fit the pieces into any predetermined state. It leaves you standing in and as absolute uncertainty, knowing you know nothing at all, that this thing you call life is not what you thought it to be, nor close to anything you could imagine.

Experiencing, be it resistance or surrender, is the vehicle, the sacred means, the candle, the light, and the darkness. It is the mystery, and the sleuth jumping up and down, pointing once again to the reality that there truly is no one who resists, and nothing substantial worth resisting.

CHAPTER 27

Death Throes

Death is the material world's boogeyman, and aging signals its approach. It's not taken too seriously when you are in your twenties unless your story is intertwined with illness, but once you cross the threshold of the forties the fear begins amping up.

This fear is the foundation of all sales pitches, not just the ones designed to make you feel good about yourself like cosmetics and plastic surgery, but everything on the market. Fear's inherent primacy is simply more visible when it targets your inability to control that new wrinkle, when its main function is to perpetuate the illusion that it is possible to escape the inescapable guest on your calendar.

Death is one of the great fallacies, perhaps the top one. It is an unavoidable outcome of a separate self, and like the separate self, it too is not quite real.

When you die, contrary to accepted opinion, you don't miss a beat, for you have not died. The body has merely passed into legend.

There's a dragonfly in my cosmic soup

Kenny and I were driving south on Highway 101, headed back to our sailboat in Mexico from a trip up north. As I often did, I was meditating in the passenger seat, and upon opening my eyes I saw an iridescent blue dragonfly smash into the windshield. That should have been the end of that beautiful creature, but it wasn't. The dragonfly didn't miss a single winged beat as it flew right through the glass. It zoomed past my ear and exited through the truck's closed back window. The blue beauty was in form, but it was not solid any more.

Is something similar happening around us all the time? Are we simply not present enough to see it?

Thirteen years later Ken died and if I had been truly present, present to life as it is without my resistance to his death, I would have seen him step out of his body and walk over to my side, put his hand on my cheek and kiss me goodbye. I was not present. I was grieving deeply, caught in the throes of loss, my stories of what was and would not be, and missed his precious exit.

However, I did experience the tail end of his departure from the visible realm. Several hours after his death a whisper of grey smoke rose from the top of his head, a clearing of his crown chakra. It was faint, but not so faint that I missed it. Beholding my lover for the last time in this incarnation, I clearly saw what felt like a display of honor for a life well lived.

Death opens a door you can walk right through …

When someone dies, they disappear from the sight of those still residing in separation. If you didn't believe in separation, if all the beliefs stabilizing the illusion had been seen through, you would see that this apparently substantial world is but the skin of an infinite onion. The death of a loved one is an immaculate opportunity when you are willing and capable of experiencing it fully.

You are always present to something, but often you are not present to *What Is*. You are not truly available as long as any scrap of identity remains, as long as the separate self still reigns. You are present to, and living as that scrap of identity. I was present as the grieving wife, the one left behind, the holder of intense personal loss. Separation had its hooks in me. The loss had set the barb ever more deeply.

Being present, fully experiencing, is not about what *was*. It is not about the absence that *will be*. Those are layered stories about *What Is*.

Fully experiencing is *now*, empty of all requirements for life to behave any way other than it is.

Stories place you in the loops of thought, installing veils around essential *Presence*. Genuine *Presence* is wide open, is the willingness to feel it all as it wafts through the form, the raw unprocessed grief and anger included.

Death is a pointer, not a dead end ...

Through years of heartache I have found that I can grieve absolutely in the middle of loss, that I do not need to escape this moment in any way. The body grieves naturally without need of prompts. Staying put, experiencing all the intensities of life without the stories of loss, opens into edgeless, bottomless, unguarded, unqualified sensation—basic unfiltered experiencing, life, *as it is*, experienced directly. It is a sacred giving-way, and because it is not resisted the feelings pass through unhindered.

Death is one of life's precious pointers. The permanence of loss kneads the heart in ways only death can, prying open the tightly shut intellect that believes it knows what is right and true. A softness replaces the hardheaded practicality, the senseless materiality, and makes it possible for a bigger truth to emerge. For a little while, the struts are knocked out from under the house of certainty, leaving gaping holes, matchstick rubble, and infinite possibilities.

Death is your friend. It is nothing to fear. It is a way-shower, a truth-sayer, a thinner of veils. Do not believe what you have been taught. It is a lie.

CHAPTER 28

Perception of Light

Light overlaid by thoughts and beliefs coalesces as the perception of a world; the world and everything in it is shimmering light, flickering prisms of experiencing.

Having experienced this many times, I realize that it is more than pretty words. A year after Kenny died, as I drove east on Highway 14 along the Columbia River, I looked out over the water and saw Ken at the wheel of our sailboat. We had sold the sailboat shortly after we returned from Mexico. *Phantasm* had been gone a long time, so seeing her clearly as she made headway on the water was a bit of a surprise. I saw her distinctly, as clear as the photograph a friend snapped years before as we sailed up the river.

I had seen Ken one other time since his death. That time he was full of life, balancing in a tree in the orchard as he pruned the branches. Walking down the long driveway towards the mailbox, the moment I saw him it felt like a bomb exploded. The blast wave from it hit me head-on and stopped my forward momentum, making me stumble.

This time was powerful too. He had a big grin on his face and while it was a calm day, the wind on the water was blowing hard, whipping up the waves. Kenny was having a grand time, the ride of his life. My heart opened and embraced his smile, his joy, and the majesty of it flattened my mind. The bottom instantly dropped out of the ruins of my world.

When I turned to look back at the road, the road and the trees lining both sides of it were gone. Everything recognizable had simply vanished, replaced by prismatic pixelated light. There was literally nothing of form and shape remaining. Amazingly, I didn't have trouble driving the winding road, even though there was no road to see, let alone drive upon. The bewitching perception lasted fifteen or twenty seconds, long enough to convince me that it was more real than what I was calling reality.

And no … drugs were not involved … unless you consider love a drug.

Clear away ideas and beliefs so that you can see

It was only years later, as more of the mystery revealed itself, that I had a clue as to what I experienced.

You see through the medium of your beliefs, as if you donned colored glasses embedded with your particular set of suppositions and projections.

Before you put on the glasses you were clear innocent experiencing, child-like openness. Looking through the lenses of belief the innocence faded until at last it died, replaced by ideas of what this is, what you are, ideas that keep you from seeing what really is.

These glasses are implants, you cannot put them on and take them off at will. They are built-in, starting with the first game your mother played with you—*you baby, me momma.*

You can't place these glasses on the bedside table and tuck the beliefs away. At night though, many of your beliefs collapse, so perhaps in the nighty-night sense you do, but it is neither conscious nor does it immutably alter what you perceive. You cannot discard your lenses, but the prescription does change. The prescription is specified by your beliefs and it changes in parallel with shifts in understanding—shifts brought about by life itself.

It's tricky...

You cannot trust your eyes to show you what is. Your eyes see what your programs tell them to see. You see what you believe, down to the most minor details of life.

You see the appearance of trees and roads, rivers and mountains, when no such thing is actually present. You see houses and fields, skyscrapers and bicycles, strangers and loved ones. You see objects in time and space, a scrap of what's here, for what you see is crystallized light colored by imaginary beliefs.

What you see is what your experience has prepared you to see.

Actuality is shimmering light, spectacularly infused shapes and textures, fractalized dimensionality, grace-filled vibrating splendor, colors so brilliant and mysterious they defy the senses, and defy definition. My words are but a child's sloppy fingerpainting displayed next to a Monet. You are the Monet. This is the Monet. This world is made of such beauty that words could never approach its grandeur.

You see a fingerpainting, rather than the true resplendence of what you experience, because you are looking through the lens of intellect. You do not see *What Is*, what your experience will show you if only you are truly ready, the actual verifiable experience, the light shimmering within and without, the light that you downgrade and call life.

Skip the show and go straight to experiencing ...

Rather than experiencing trees and roads, friends and strangers, look closely at perception itself. You think you know what it is. You don't. If you did, you'd be howling at the moon, praising the love that flows through every atom of this illusory life.

Knowing places the veil over your eyes, creating separation where there is none. Ignored and overlooked, *Isness* doesn't go anywhere. There truly isn't a veil, other than as an appearance in aliveness itself. *This* is always right here, right now, is ever present and freely accessible in every breath of experience. There is nothing it is not.

Sound ... taste ... sight ... touch ... smell ... any one of them will show you the way. Slow down and feel into the sound of the wind as it blows through your hair, or the sound within what seems to be the silence. Feel the aliveness in a bite of juicy orange. Imbibe that whispery cloud; inhale it; touch into it; lay down on the grass and let yourself fall into the sky. Sense the tingling sensation of your finger on the keyboard, or your foot as it rests upon the floor. Make love in a slow sizzle, relishing each stroke of your partner's fingers. Smell is fun, especially when the smell is unreasonably present, a memory of smell, like your grandfather's pipe or the smell of bread baking in the oven ... or close your eyes and explore the world of wonder you think of as a black nothing.

Even though it's not real in the way you think, it isn't nothing ...

Nothing is nothing. There is always more to see if you are willing to put aside what you think you know. Whatever you do, do it and it alone. Give yourself over to it completely. See what happens when you treat your experience, whatever it is, with rapt attention like a new lover.

You move so fast. You don't stop and smell the roses. Engage with your experience with all your heart. Experience is something you move through like a sleepwalker, thinking it's all the same thing over and over, night after night. Experience is never the same, not from day to day, nor moment to moment. It is always in motion, flickering in and out of manifestation, only seeming to take the same shape and form because that's what you believe it will do.

Experiencing is alive but what you see is not. You see *Infinite Aliveness* wearing the coat of many colors, the myths and traditions, your assumptions, ideologies, and identities—the narratives you trust.

It doesn't have to be that way. Seize the day; truly experience your experience. Your experience exactly as it is right now is the portal beyond time and space, the key to the unlocked gate.

You are magnificence itself ...

There is nothing wrong with you. There is no demon to exorcise, nothing in need of a fix. You have never made a mistake. That would be impossible. You, exactly as you are, are this, are simple experiencing, mirroring your mostly hidden beliefs. You have always been this. Life's splendid mystery eludes you because you trust in the fallacies. That's all. That illusion is the only thing standing in your way of recognizing what you are, and it is pure fiction, nothing you can overcome, conquer, or annihilate, for it is nothing at all.

Isn't it worth taking a look?

What if everything you have believed, and that you still believe, is based on a lie? What would mirror back to you if everything you think you know disintegrated and you found yourself standing naked before the unfolding now? It will happen when your body passes into legend. That's a given, so why wait? I promise it is well worth the risk to live in the world as *Infinite Aliveness*, to be truly alive, profoundly awake while dreaming.

About Amaya Gayle

Amaya laughs when anyone asks for a bio. There is no appropriate bio for her or anyone. It's impossible to write one when every word points to a material world, the inevitable failing of language that relies on nouns. Life isn't a noun. It's closer to a verb but even that isn't the truth.

She, like you, doesn't exist other than as an expression of consciousness itself. Talking about her in biographical terms is a disservice to the truth, and to anyone who might be led to believe in such nonsense, to use what they read as a comparison point, a measuring stick, or heaven forbid, a map to the promised land.

None of us exist, all of us exist, but not in the way we think. Happily, *Actuality* is much better than we can imagine. Looking at her, you would swear this is a lie. She's there after all, but honestly, she's not ... and she is. Appearances are deceiving.

Ideas spring into words. Words flow and yet no one writes them. Fingers placed on the keyboard, words simply appear. Don't you love a paradox! Life is nothing, if not paradoxical.

Bios usually wax on about accomplishments and beliefs, happenings in time and space. She has never accomplished anything, has no beliefs, and like you was never born and will never die.

To contact Amaya Gayle: amayag@amayagayle.com
Website: www.amayagayle.com

www.ingramcontent.com/pod-product-compliance
Lightning Source LLC
LaVergne TN
LVHW041937070526
838199LV00051BA/2827